Contents

Chapter 4

Chapter 5

Introduction

At the time of writing, we are facing yet another major crisis. This time it's a pandemic, Covid-19, that has swept across the world forcing economies to shut down. Financial markets collapsed as they tried to absorb the implications for prices and the broader economy. Fiscal and monetary stimulus, on a scale never seen before, helped markets recover much of their immediate losses. The battle is against time to find a vaccine before untold damage occurs. The optimistic view is that a "V-shaped" recovery will be more likely. However, many economists and analysts fear that the road to recovery will not take effect immediately. These are truly uncertain times presenting big challenges to investors and even home-owners so preparedness and planning is vital.

The major asset classes, shares, bonds, and real estate have enjoyed a record-long bull market. In early 2020, despite Covid-19, valuations remain high and are not supported by the 'fundamentals'. In other words, things look over-valued given current conditions. We have also enjoyed the longest, albeit tepid, economic cycle on record, yet share values have grown at a disproportionately faster clip than the economy. Many economists argue an economic contraction and mean-reverting correction in asset prices was on the cards before the pandemic. This is supported by a yield curve inversion, a reliable predictor of recession, in August 2019. What does this all mean for the average retail investor?

The last two decades have seen two major financial market crashes, which led to significant losses for many investors. Whether we will have a third crash remains to be seen, but it is possible. How should investors navigate these turbulent and volatile periods? One answer is to avoid financial markets, but many depend on them for income in retirement. There are simple steps that can be taken to mitigate losses that don't require a PhD, or even professional help. That doesn't mean you should fire your financial advisor. It just means you can be more hands-on, even if it's only communicating more effectively with your financial advisor.

A common thread that weaves through these boom-bust cycles is monetary policy controlled by central banks. Their role has increased as the need to inject liquidity into the system to prevent economic collapse becomes ever greater. The unintended consequence has been a misallocation of capital; money is not being used by companies to invest and grow. Instead it is too often being used to buy back shares in support of increasing valuations. This has implications for risk-return methodologies since high valuations increases volatility. Simply put, the higher values climb the further they can fall, the more anxious investors become, and the more prone they are to making impulsive decisions. This phenomenon is not limited to financial markets.

The low cost of borrowing has created excessive valuations in the real estate market. For many, homes are the only source of wealth creation, but as owners learnt after the collapse of the housing market in 2006-07, they can also be a source of misery. As an investment vehicle, real estate provides substantial returns, often out-performing financial markets. Cheap credit has encouraged speculation in pursuit of easy gains, all too often at the expense of an understanding of the risks. Over-valuations and risk have contributed to an unstable housing market with unintended consequences. A paralysis has gripped many home owners, unsure how to realize gains in home equity. High prices have pushed homes out of reach of younger buyers, which has disrupted the property ladder. Home-ownership, the American dream, has been declining. And all this despite record low borrowing rates.

While this book covers the main principles of investing such as asset allocation, diversification, risk and return, optimization, passive vs active funds, plus a chapter dedicated to real estate, I have taken care to place everything within the economic context and investing environment of more recent decades. This hopefully draws attention to areas where traditional models of investing haven't kept pace with the changing times, and where investors need to be especially vigilant.

The book is aimed at individuals with little or no previous knowledge of investing wishing to gain a basic understanding of how to invest. The book also delves into areas of investing for those wishing to pursue a deeper appreciation of the subject.

Chapter 1

Investing Environment

There are three B's that have characterized the investing environment over the last few decades; banks, bubbles and behavior. Banks have found themselves at the center of much controversy, while asset bubbles seem to have sprouted up like mushrooms, making our behavior the focus of much attention. The three B's have interacted in a way clearly playing a part in both the creation of crises and how we respond to them. This is where our story begins.

In both the US and the UK, there has been an era of deregulation starting with the UK in 1986 with the 'Big Bang', followed by the repeal of Glass-Steagall Act in the US, in 1999. In the UK, there was a liberalization of markets prior to 1986, such as the relaxation of exchange controls and bank reserving requirements, but a big push came from the introduction of electronic trading and looser rules over commissions. In the US, the damage caused by the Great Depression made policy-makers rethink the relationship between retail and investment banking. Having one bank do both created a conflict of interest, since using depositor savings to invest in risky assets was unpalatable, especially after the stock market crash in 1929. This all changed in 1999, and retail banks were once again allowed to speculate with risky assets.

Banks complained the old model of using savings to lend was no longer profitable. Customers' savings were a primary source for bank lending. But that money could be withdrawn by deposit holders without notice. Lending, on the other hand, is a long-term commitment so this created a balance sheet problem. Short-term cash demand was inconsistent with long term loans, giving rise to the notion of maturity transformation. Assets were not covering liabilities. To fund more lending, banks needed another source of revenue and found it in charging commissions and fees from trading in financial markets.

The dot.com bubble in 2001, followed shortly after the liberalization of financial markets and was technology driven. It was a classic bubble in the sense that share values of technology companies were fueled by overly-optimistic expectations of futures earnings. The housing bubble that sparked the credit crisis leading to the Great Recession in 2008-2009, had its origins in financial markets. Asset valuations in 2020, has led many analysts and economists to speculate we were in another bubble fueled by monetary policy.

High inflation in the UK in the 1970's, led to a strong monetary response from the Bank of England, the central bank. High short-term interest rates were introduced to tighten the money supply and curb inflationary pressures. A similar picture emerged in the late 1970's in the US, where inflation reached double digits. The Federal Reserve Bank's response was to raise the federal funds rate, the short-term interbank lending rate, to very significant levels. Tightening the money supply tamed inflation, but the prospect of deflation began to emerge in the late 1980's, which led to a lowering of interest rates. This trend continued after both the 1987 and dot.com stock market crashes. Fast forward to 2020, and the surge in money supply as measured by M2 has quadrupled in a decade and has many economists contemplating the return of the ever-elusive inflation.

Monetary tinkering has created controversy over what the role of central banks should be. Many believe it should be primarily concerned with inflation and employment. Yet evidence has been mounting that central banks have been shoring up financial markets. There is debate over whether this apparent gift to markets is an unintended consequence of central bank operations, or a calculated and acceptable trade-off to help the overall economy. What is clear is all asset classes show signs of an inverse relationship to interest rates. As interest rates fall asset prices rise and vice versa. While this inverse relationship has always been tied to bonds, it is also visible in share values and home prices. Share values are affected because they are tied to a discount rate that is applied to future cash flows. Lower interest rates also feed into mortgage rates allowing buyers to borrow more pushing up home prices.

Behind the scenes there were changes in lending business models. Recent decades have seen banks moving more and more into mortgage lending and investing in financial markets. Mortgages, when wrapped into securities and sold on, were profitable. These are known as mortgage backed securities (MBS) and the process is called securitization. Other forms of debt were also being sold on in a similar way. These were known as collateralized debt obligations (CDOs).

The US mortgage market is largely underwritten by Government Sponsored Entities (GSEs), with Fannie Mae and Freddie Mac being the biggest. One of their functions is to create mortgage backed securities. Being quasi-government bodies, they are considered relatively benign, or risk-free entities. However, the problem with collateralized mortgage loans really began when the private sector entered this securitization market. By combining and packaging mortgages across the risk spectrum into one security risk is mitigated. For the model to work, home prices had to grow. But this didn't happen. In 2006, home prices reached unsustainable levels. The riskiest tranche, known as subprime mortgages, began to default, which gave rise to a credit freeze. Toxic loans had created an atmosphere of mistrust between lenders as nobody knew who was holding them. The credit crisis had begun.

The fiscal and monetary response from governments and central banks was unprecedented. The financial system had to be saved at any costs to avoid an economic depression. Failing corporations were bailed out by governments, while central banks went on a bond buying spree, known as Quantitative Easing

(QE). QE involves buying large quantities of bonds creating a dearth of supply that pushes up bond prices. Since bond prices and interest rate have an inverse relationship, borrowing becomes cheaper. The sellers of the bonds would then use the funds from the sale of bonds to invest in plant and productive capacity. This in turn would spur growth and stimulate the economy. Well, that is what was supposed to have happened.

The low cost of capital was being put to other uses. One of these uses was leveraged share buy-backs that artificially increase the value of a company's shares by removing those shares from its balance sheet. This increases the earnings per share making the company look more profitable. That in turn attracts more investment pushing up values even more. Managers who have share options in their companies benefit directly from this increase in value, thereby creating a conflict of interest. An unintended consequence of monetary policy has been higher asset prices at the cost of lower productivity. Monetary policy and the economy were misaligned and financial markets were not bridging the divide. A more direct duopolistic causation between central bank accommodation and financial markets was emerging. Markets were becoming dependent on monetary policy being supportive of asset values.

At the time of writing, the low rate environment continues to affect all major asset classes. As of February, 2020 the Case Shiller Index (US home price index) is 17% higher than its 2006 peak in nominal terms, and up nearly 60% from its trough in 2012. Historically, home prices have remained within the range of 3-4 times median annual income. During the housing bubble that ratio was over 5 times median annual income. Correspondingly, the S&P 500 Index is up 300% from its trough in 2009 and bonds have lost between 30-40% of their dividend yield. In the UK, the Land Registry shows the average house price has increased 21% from its peak in 2007. Those are astonishing feats given the destruction caused by the downturn a decade earlier and can largely be explained by record low interest rates. If you plotted interest rates and asset prices on a chart you will see that a prolonged period of declining interest rates has coincided with a commensurate increase in asset values.

So why is this all relevant to the investor? It is against the background of unprecedented stimulus and looser financial regulations that investors need ask questions and formulate their investing decisions. Is it a great time to pile into investments when valuations seem excessively out of kilter with the norm? Or, have we entered a new normal where valuations needed to be reassessed based on current market values. Is it the case asset prices can't be allowed to correct because of the damage it will cause if prices revert to the mean? It begs the question; have central banks been digging themselves into an ever-deepening hole with no clear exit strategy? Proponents of supply-side economics and efficient markets will argue it's all par for the course. Keynesian economists will argue there is not enough stimulus. Investors, in the meantime, must grapple with the increased uncertainty.

Two other features of this changing landscape are worthy a mention; an increasingly interconnected world and behavioral sciences. Asset bubbles and monetary stimulus are not restricted to the English-speaking world. Much of Europe and Asia also have also seen out-sized asset price increases influences by low interest rate policies. Banks and corporations operate across borders, while fiscal and monetary ideas are mirrored across the globe. In the meantime, financial behaviorists have been gaining recognition while providing answers to questions about the nature of risk, investing, and financial excesses. They posit humans have an inherent 'herd' mentality. Individuals tend to follow the path chosen by the many believing the herd must be right. While this impulse seems rational, behaviorists point to evidence that following the herd doesn't necessarily lead to good outcomes. In fact, doing the very opposite of the herd has become an increasingly popular adjunct to an investment strategy.

What is investing?

Investing is no different from any other kind of transaction involving the exchange of money. You exchange your hard-earned money for a product. In the case of shares, you buy ownership of a small piece of a company. With bonds, you buy the right to a stream of income and the return of your principal. The price of financial assets—as with anything—is determined by supply and demand. As people scramble to buy products prices goes up. When everyone wants to sell, price goes down. Demand and supply, for the most part, remains in a sort of equilibrium. Financial markets behave in a similar way, but prices fluctuate more wildly since they are intangibles having no easily discernible intrinsic value. This is the most confusing aspect of investing. Things can change out of the blue. Investments can gain value one day and lose all those gains the next day. There is an apparent randomness to price fluctuations for the most part. Markets are shaped by the desire to make money, euphoria, loss, risk, volatility, and uncertainty. The market feeds on itself.

Uncertainty is a behavioral trait often a response to another behavior. A study of how we behave can tell us a lot about what makes us react to things the way we do, and ultimately whether those reactions are doing us good or harm. Knowing yourself and how other investors behave provides an invaluable insight in how to respond to events. Knowing what kinds of events trigger behaviors can be useful in shaping the responses to it. In times of heightened uncertainty and volatility attitudes towards risk change. For example, rolling out of riskier asset classes through fear, but leaving it too late can lead to regret.

A distinction needs to be made between investors and traders. Investors buy and hold their investments for the long term. They want their investments to grow consistently. For example, retirees needing income, and companies needing to expand their businesses invest to satisfy long-term goals. Traders, on the other hand, buy and sell investments to make a profit over the short term. They trade frequently taking advantage of small price movements. This requires a lot of skill and often produces disappointing results. What investors and traders share in common is the inevitable trade-off between 'risk and return'. The relationship between 'risk and return' is fundamental to any investment as they are inextricably linked. The greater the return, the greater the risk. The smaller the risk the lower the returns. This is because investor demand a greater return for accepting more risk. They want to be adequately compensated for the risks they take.

Buying shares and bonds is no different to buying anything else. You go to a market, check the price and part with your money in exchange for a product. You can do this yourself, or pay for the services of a financial advisor to do it for you. If you use a financial advisor, you are paying that person for their expertise to manage your investments for you. If you manage your own investments, it is paramount you understand the principles of investing. In fact, it is important to understand investing basics even if you choose to use a professional. This is not so that you can tell your advisor what to do if things go wrong—and they will go wrong—but to communicate more effectively your goals and attitudes towards risk. Being able to speak the same financial language will benefit your portfolio.

So, what are bonds and shares? When you buy a share, you are buying a small piece of a company that gives you the right to a share in its profits. Buying a bond is the equivalent to making a loan to an entity. These bond-issuing entities can be either a company, or a government. In other words, they are borrowing from you and agree to pay you a fixed amount at regular intervals. They also agree to pay back your principal on a fixed date. For retail investors, buying individual bonds and shares is not practical because it is time consuming and costly. Moreover, it could lead to a portfolio that is undiversified, therefore, exposed to undue risk. The golden rule of investing is never place all your eggs in one basket. Luckily, the work is already done for investors in the form is funds. They exist both for shares and bonds. Investors simply invest in a fund and enjoy all the benefits of securities selection and diversification.

Diversification

Putting all your eggs into one basket is the worst thing you can do in investing. By investing all your money in one or two companies you concentrate the risk of losses considerably. Even a random selection of shares in, say, ten companies would provide a better risk-adjusted return than the shares of one carefully selected company. By spreading shares over a large pool of companies you diversify away risk. When one company performs poorly it won't have a big drag on a portfolio consisting of many company shares. Furthermore, by selecting shares that move in opposite directions to each other, risk is greatly reduced. For example, shares in a company that sells umbrellas won't do well in the summer, but shares in a company that sells cold drinks will do well. They have what is called a negative correlation and this is discussed in more detail in Chapter 2. There is a school of thought that posits the benefits of diversification are limited beyond a certain threshold of pooled shares. Other theories claim that the broader the diversification the better. Whichever is correct, diversification is an investors best friend.

Portfolio Construction

Asset Allocation
Asset allocation is deciding how much to invest in each of the asset classes, which will be mostly either shares or bonds. It is the most important first step. The industry standard is 60% into shares and 40% in bonds for most investors. Shares provide growth and bonds provide income. By spreading investments across these two asset classes, risk is minimized since they are negatively correlated. That is, they move in opposite directions. When share prices decline in value, bonds will offer a cushion as they are less volatile and even increase in value as investors seek their safety. At least that is the theory. In practice, this doesn't always happen. In recent years, the correlation between shares, bonds, and other asset classes has changed. They tend to move more in tandem. The main point to remember is that asset allocation contributes 90% to returns.

Selection
Having decided on asset allocation, the next step is asset selection. This involves selecting the shares,

bonds, or funds you want to invest in. This process contributes only 5% to portfolio performance, but nevertheless is a very important step. The process is complicated by the vast array of investments on offer. Most retail investors will be selecting between funds. Broadly, they fall into two categories; those which are professionally managed called 'active' funds and those that are not managed called 'passive' index funds. Actively managed funds are mutual funds, and passive index funds are ETFs (Exchange Traded Funds). There is some cross-over between the two.

So how do you choose between the two? There is considerable debate about whether actively managed, or passive index funds provide better returns. A large body of research shows that when fees are deducted from managed funds, their returns are no better than those for passive funds. While this may be true for share funds, bond funds benefit from being managed for a variety of reasons. For example, bonds are not as actively bought and sold so are less liquid, which means finding buyers can be harder. In defense of actively-managed funds, managers point out all the research they do, from which investors benefit. They also make the arguments that passive funds hug an index so don't have the flexibility to reduce exposure to loss making companies, or sectors if markets change. The bottom line is choice should be determined by consistent performance.

Timing

The third and final step, called timing, is deciding when to invest. This is probably one of the most controversial aspects of investing as many professional investors believe it does not matter when you invest because markets are in a continual state of flux, going up and down. Trying to time the market, therefore, is very difficult to do with any degree of success. There are though different kinds of timing considerations. For example, you may not have a lump sum to invest, so will be allocating a fixed amount from your wages at regular intervals. There may be other life events or expenses that need funding such as college or big ticket items. You may be close to retirement and will be more dependent on fixed income so want to avoid exposing yourself to unnecessary risk. Generally, it is thought 'timing' contributes the least of the three steps to overall portfolio performance.

In a nutshell, asset allocation, securities selection, and timing is all that needs doing. Investing 60% in a 'passive', well diversified index fund, and 40% in a well-diversified, managed bond fund is all that is required for a basic portfolio. The only ongoing task will be to ensure you keep those percentages constant. This is called portfolio rebalancing and is achieved by selling and buying stocks and bonds within the portfolio until you're back to a 60/40 asset allocation. And you may only need to do this once or twice a year. For example, if your share fund has increased in value it will now be more than 60% of your total, so your bonds will now represent less than 40%. You will need to sell some of your shares and use that cash to buy more bonds until you are back where you started.

Younger investors may like to consider target date funds, that do the whole process for you based on your time horizon. Initially, the portfolio will be stacked towards equities to gain growth, and will gradually incorporate more bonds the closer you are to retirement.

Passive vs Active

There is a compelling argument for investing in passive index funds over actively-managed funds. Few fund managers consistently beat their benchmark because of fees. As a consequence, money has poured into index fund leading to a rapid growth in ETFs, which makes some pundits nervous. It should also be remembered they are a relatively recent innovation, and merely mimic or track an index, so may lose out on mispricing opportunities from which actively managed funds derive benefit.

A popular index is the S&P 500. It contains 500 of the largest companies in the US, so acts as the benchmark for the market. However, it is heavily weighted towards a small number of large technology companies. This can distort the performance of the index. If valuations of technology companies are very high compared to other sectors, a correction in tech stocks may be a drag on the index.

Putting It All Together

Buying financial investments is like buying anything else. You go to a store, select your items, and pay for them. You may prefer to go to a large online supermarket to get better deals. You can do the same with investments. These financial supermarkets are often discount brokers and are widely used. Fidelity, TD Ameritrade and Charles Schwab are good examples. There are also online Robo Advisors such as Betterment that are technology driven and automate the process.

Having selected an online platform, you will need to open an account, called a trading account, which can often be done online. You will then need to add funds to your account from your regular checking or savings account. Once funds are sitting in your trading account, follow the menu options for trading. You will see input boxes requiring a ticker symbol, number of shares, sell or buy, and order type. Order type allows you to pay using a market order, which is the prevailing market price. You can also choose a limit order, which allows you to choose the price you want to pay, and will be fulfilled when the price is met. It is important to become familiar with the order types and the functions they provide. For example, a stop loss is a very useful tool for traders who want to minimize losses. You enter a price below which a sell order will be automatically triggered.

You will need to know the ticker symbol for your selected funds. For your shares allocation, this might be an ETF that tracks an index such as the S&P 500, such as SPY. For your bond allocation, it might be a broadly diversified managed fund, such as AGG. A useful source for selecting funds is Morningstar, which rates many funds by performance. It also offers a lot of other useful information. While it is a subscription service, some of the information is provided at no charge. Some funds have written reports justifying the ratings given to the them. So, a lot of the work has been done for you making the selection of funds much easier. You may find the online trading platform you have chosen also provides useful information. Using more than one source of information during the selection process will help reaffirm your choice.

To recap, asset allocation builds performance and diversification mitigates risk. Buying quality passive index funds and re-balancing the portfolio at intervals maintains your risk profile. All things being equal, this is all you need to do. The rest of the book goes into more details about investment theory. There is also a chapter devoted to real estate. If you are following the DIY investing route it is recommended you read the other chapters. While I endeavor to fill in many of the gaps, the book is not a substitute for using a financial advisor. While it offers tips towards independence, the book will also assist in communicating more effectively with a financial advisor.

Chapter 2

The last chapter looked at the investment process at its most basic level. This chapter will look under the hood to see what mechanisms are at play and how they might offer more guidance to investing. We will look at ways of measuring performance, introduce investing concepts, and look at the role behavior plays in the choices we make. First, a more detailed description of the major assets classes is warranted.

ETFs and Mutual Funds

As mentioned in the previous chapter, most individual investors will be investing in funds as opposed to individual shares or bonds. This is because funds are diversified into a pool of investments to minimize risk. The investment strategy is typically for investors who buy and hold. They are investing over the long term and are not trading frequently with the aim of trying to exploit small, short-term price differences. Funds are spilt up into two main categories; actively managed and passive. Actively managed funds use research to determine companies that perform well. Investors invest in a mutual fund in much the same way as they buy shares. Unlike shares which trade throughout the day, mutual funds only trade at the end of each day. Since they are actively managed, they incur fees. Only trading at the end of the day has implications for valuations. ETFs are usually passively managed and track an index. Their fees are lower so can compete with managed funds, offering comparable returns. They also trade more like shares, meaning they can be bought and sold throughout the day.

There are two types of mutual fund; open-end funds (OEF) and closed-end funds (CEF). Open-ended are so called because they are open to issue more shares as demand for them increases. They are typically what we mean when we talk about mutual funds. Closed end funds are closed in the sense they issue a set number of shares. They trade in a similar way to ETFs. Open-end funds are considered less risky than closed-end funds, whereas the latter can produce higher returns.

Since ETFs trade like shares, theoretically, they may provide opportunities to find mispricing, but this is not something buy and hold investors engage in often. Apart from lower fees, ETFs also have a tax advantage over mutual funds (which incur capital gains), so they are considered more 'tax friendly'. ETFs offer the best of everything so are a compelling choice. There are managed ETFs, although they are less common. The competition between active and passive funds has led to a fee war. Mutual funds have lowered their fees to win back business lost to passive ETFs, which is en-couraging news for the retail investor. A final note of caution regarding mutual funds fees is that they can impose "loads". These are fees that are charged on entering, or exiting a fund. Funds with these loads are best avoided.

When it comes to bonds, the consensus is that actively managed bond funds are a better choice. This is mainly due to the way index funds allocate capital based on market capitalization. Bonds are a different animal and reflect the indebtedness, or borrowings of a company. Companies with high levels of debt are not always seen as a good thing, so selecting funds with good credit risk, and reputable management is important. For fee-conscious investors, some actively managed bond funds do have low fees, so remain competitive with their passive counterparts. Bond indexes are generally thought to be unreliable, which may have implications for bond funds that track them. This runs somewhat counter to the notion of bonds being more efficiently priced than shares, but it may have something to do with the illiquidity of the bond market. Bonds are not as actively traded as shares, so finding buyers isn't as fluid.

As mentioned already, funds are comprised of pooled investments. As such it is important to understand what goes into them. Shares are sometimes called equities, securities, or stocks. When you buy a share, you are buying a small piece of a company that pays you a share of net profits in proportion to the number of shares you own. That payment is called a dividend and is not a fixed amount because profits fluctuate. Share values also fluctuate in line with investor expectations of future growth. When changes in share value is added to dividend yield, you arrive at a total return number. This tells the investors the total gain (or loss) made. If dividend yield is poor, or a company doesn't pay a dividend, increased share value compensates the investor.

New technology companies may offer substantial growth but little to no dividend. That is because profits are ploughed back into developing existing products and innovating new products for future expansion. Mature 'blue chip' companies offer both dividend and growth, while other companies such as utilities pay reliable dividends but don't offer as much growth.

Shares

The most common type of share is aptly named an 'ordinary' share. While investors in ordinary shares are entitled to a share in the profits, the final decision to pay a dividend resides with the company. The only sway shareholders have over a company is voting rights. If you own a majority of shares you effectively have control over a company. The downside to owning shares is you are last in line if things go wrong and a company goes into liquidation. That means you may lose all the money you invested in the company. It is the risk you accepted when you invested in the company.

Preference shares are a little like bonds. They pay a fixed rate and are redeemed on a set date. If a company goes into liquidation, preference shares—as their name suggests—are higher in the pecking order than ordinary shares. In addition, they have priority over ordinary shares in dividend payments. Preference shares can be converted to ordinary shares.

Shares provide better returns over the long term than any other asset class. From 1929, $1 in cash would have given you $20 over an 80-year period. Investing $1 in shares over the same period would have given you $1,262. If the market had been perfectly timed the returns would have been astronomically higher. However, imperfect timing is the best we can hope for. Shares go through periods when even cash outperforms them. Over a three-year period, cash outperforms shares about 30% of the time. Governments bonds outperform shares over a three to five-year period. In fact, share only come solidly into their own over an 18-year period. It is why timing the market is so difficult to do, and a buy-and-hold strategy is so important.

Bonds

Bonds are different to shares. Investors are not buying a small piece of a company. They are lending to an entity, such as a company or a government in return for an income stream and the return of principal at a fixed date. Government bonds are generally considered 'risk free' as the default risk is lower than for corporate bonds. Some government bonds are linked to inflation. These are known as TIPs, and provide both income and principal protection against inflation. As prices of goods and services increase, so do the value and income of inflation-linked bonds. This makes them an attractive option, especially for retirees, since both credit risk and inflation risk are small.

Bonds pay a fixed interest and have a maturity date when the bond is redeemed and original principle is paid back. When bonds are first issued, they are sold at par value of $100 per bond and sold in denominations of $1,000. Bonds can fluctuate in value when, for example, interest rates change. Generally, when interest rates go up, bond values decline. Bonds have what is called an 'inverse' relationship with interest rates, which is fundamental to understanding how they work. This becomes especially poignant in a low interest rate environment, since yields can be meagre and investors no longer adequately rewarded.

Bonds are often traded above par value. This lowers the quoted coupon rate, which no longer indicates a meaningful yield. Given that bond yields change and mature at different intervals, various measures are used to indicate to investors what they can expect. This is where things get a little complicated. If a bonds value has increased, it won't be paying the coupon rate otherwise the borrower would be saddled with unrealistic interest payments. So, the coupon rate is measured against the current value and this gives us the 'current yield', which is a more accurate measure of the yield of a bond as it changes value. The total return of a bond is its redemption value plus income yield. This is known as the redemption yield—redemption refers to the date a bond matures. This gives an indication of whether the bond has made a gain, or a loss. If the redemption value is lower than current market price of a bond, it has made a loss and vice versa.

Inflation also effects bond values and is measured by yield to maturity. The 'duration' of a bond is measured in years and measures how long it would take to pay back the bond with coupon payments together with principal. Duration is used to measure a bond's sensitivity to interest rates. The higher the duration the greater a bond's value will fluctuate up or down.

Bonds are safer, or carry less risk, than shares. It is for that reason that they are used to buttress a portfolio against volatility. When valuations in shares fluctuate wildly, investors will often flee to the safety of bonds, which pushes up their value and protects the portfolio. Bonds are said to have a negative correlation to shares. At least, that is the theory. In recent times, as interest rates have declined to record low levels, there is evidence that the upward pressure on bond values has made them behave in a similar way to shares. In other words, instead of moving in opposite directions, bonds and shares move together. When shares go down in value, so do bonds and vice versa.

In the event a company becomes insolvent and goes into liquidation, bond holders are higher in the pecking order than shareholders. However, most bonds don't offer a hedge against inflation. Bonds with longer maturities carry more inflation risk, interest rate risk, and default risk, so will offer higher yields to compensate investors. The investor will want to know that he is being compensated not just for these risks, but that the yield is higher than the risk-free rate of a government bond. The risk-free rate offers a comparatively low rate because the risk of a government defaulting on its loans is generally low.

Placing bonds and yields in their current context is vital in helping investors navigate the fraught relationship they sometimes have with the economy and markets. Years of declining interest rates imposed by central banks have compressed yields to a point where investors are not being adequately compensated for the risk they take. The ten-year US Treasury bond stood at half a percentage point in August, 2002. When inflation is taken into account, the yield can become negative. Investors are effectively paying the US government to lend to them. This is of course very good for governments since their debt is inflated away. Low rates have in turn pushed up bond values. While that may be a redeeming factor, bonds have lost their fixed income appeal. Their function for many investors is primarily that of providing a dependable fixed income. Investors either accept the need to pay considerably more to obtain the required income, or buy into riskier bonds and other asset classes to capture the required yield. This has forced many investors into investments outside their normal risk profiles, and it has also created a chase for yield of global proportions. This has yet fully to play out and is a big unknown.

As with shares, managing a portfolio of individual bonds is not recommended for the novice investor. Well diversified bond funds can be easily purchased. Since bond funds contain a variety of bond types with different durations and yields, valuation is complex. You cannot buy a bond fund at par with a fixed maturity date with the knowledge your principal will be returned. They are ongoing entities and fluctuate in price and yield. The only yardstick to measure value is the yield, or distribution rate. Buying into a bond fund with a comparatively low yield means the fund may be overvalued. If interest rates rise, a bond fund will lose value. The relationship between bond yields and price is referred to as convexity. A 1% rise in interest rates can result in a decline in bond value equal to maturity. For example, a 1% rise in interest rates for a bond with a three-year maturity would lead to a 3% decline in value., and so on. However, a decline in interest rates affects bond values less that a rise in rates. Also, note that progressive interest rate rises have a diminishing effect on values. The more they rise, the less values decline. This relationship is referred to a convexity. Buying into bond funds when they offer better yields thus lower prices would seem prudent. Having an in-dividually managed bond portfolio may offer the best of everything, but expect to pay for it.

Portfolio Theory

A portfolio is constructed by investing in asset classes in varying proportions to match an individual's risk profile and financial needs. Portfolio a security's per-formance and correlation. Correlations show how dif-ferent share values move in parallel, or in opposite di-rections. Different sectors of the economy are affected by different factors. For example, when sunscreen is selling well due to hot weather, wooly hats won't be selling well. Shares in companies selling sunscreen and wooly hats will be negatively correlated. If you only bought shares in sunscreen you will lose money in win-ter. If you own shares in both sunscreen and wooly hats they provide a hedge against each other. Portfolio theory calculates all the correlations using historic returns to maximize returns and minimize risk.

Portfolio theory doesn't restrict itself to the shares of two companies. Other shares can be added in the mix to find the optimum risk-return. However, there is a threshold beyond which adding more shares does little to improve portfolio performance. The theory is useful, however, in helping to understand the dynamics of financial markets. It also illustrates the importance of diversification, one of the bedrocks of investing. Interestingly, even ten randomly chosen shares will perform better than one individually-selected share. This is referred to as naïve selection and is not part of portfolio theory. Modern Portfolio Theory takes a different view of optimized risk-adjusted returns by combing the market with risk-free government bonds.

Modern Portfolio Theory is attributable to the economist, Harry Markowitz. It is based around the idea that markets are efficiently priced, so you cannot improve performance by stock picking. You simply buy the market, which could be a well-diversified fund that tracks an index such as the S&P 500. All specific risk is then diversified away and you are left with only systematic risk. Specific risk relates to risk inherent within companies, whereas systematic risk is exogenous so outside the control of companies. By combining the market with risk-free government bonds, systematic risk is also reduced. The theory posits that since you can't beat the market, the only way to increase returns is by taking on more risk. This entails increasing a portfolio's asset allocation to the market, and reducing exposure to the risk-free allocation. For investors wishing to retreat to safety and sacrifice returns, they reduce market exposure and buy more governments bonds. Put simply, this means buying more equities and less bonds for greater returns, or the reverse for greater stability. It all sounds wonderfully simple and effective, so what is the catch?

Portfolio theory rests on the assumption that markets are efficient, and that all investors have access to the same information and are similarly motivated. An efficient market is where prices quickly correct because investors see opportunities and seize upon them to make a profit. The law of supply and demand comes into play, closing the window of opportunity and restoring price equilibrium. However, not all investors will be using the same information. And how does efficient pricing explain asset bubbles where prices become very disconnected from fundamentals. This seems far from efficient pricing. Bubbles do burst and prices eventually correct, but they leave a trail of destruction in their wake. If we leave aside this objection, Modern Portfolio Theory offers a mathematical model for optimizing risk-adjusted return. It also offers a method for increasing returns without trying to beat the market. So how does it work?

Optimization

Optimization is finding the maximum return with the minimum risk. It can be used for individual shares, or funds. It uses standard deviation and historical data to find the optimal risk-adjusted return. Standard deviation is a measure of risk and calculates how likely an event will deviate from its historical average. Optimized portfolios are often expressed in terms of their Sharpe ratio, which tells us by how much an investment performs above the risk-free rate. Optimization can also be used to fulfill other investment strategies such as income or growth. A criticism of optimization is that it reduces diversification, shrinking several investments to just two or three. An alternative is to use the Black-Litterman model that uses optimization, but requires investors to have a view on future returns. Since future returns are difficult to predict, the model is more useful to investors who have reliable information that supports their views. Portfoliovisualizer.com offers a free optimization online tool.

Another criticism of optimization is its use of standard deviation. The model measures risk using a symmetrical Bell Curve so assumes risk falls within certain parameters. However, these parameters don't account for high sigma events, which occur more frequently than is assumed. These events are sometimes referred to as having fat-tail risk. They don't sit comfortably on a symmetrical curve. So, when major events occur that impact markets negatively, investors are caught off guard and can suffer greater drawdowns. In addition to high sigma events, there are 'Black Swan" events.

These are events that happen quite out of the blue and can be very damaging. Since they have no precedent, they have no probability of occurring, yet we know they happen. The occurrence of Covid-19 in 2020, was thought by some to be a Black Swan event. However, such an event was anticipated within the scientific community. The key takeaway is that risk management is not given enough priority. While mathematical models offer some guidance, they don't provide fool-proof answers. Plan for the worst and hope for the best. Don't underestimate long tail risk.

Sector Rotation

A method for reducing risk during a downturn, or increasing returns in a growth period is by rotating in and out of sectors. Different sectors within the economy react differently during different parts of the economic cycle. Economies expand and contract every few years. When the economy is over-heating, the expansion period may be close to ending. Central banks will reduce the money supply to prevent inflation, a major cause of recessions. At the beginning of a recession the economy is contracting. Economic contraction and growth are measured by total national output, which is referred to as GDP (Gross Domestic Product). A technical recession is two quarters of negative growth. By 'rotating' into sectors that do well and rotating out of those sectors that perform poorly, you take advantage of the upside and reduce exposure to the downside.

When economies are over-heating natural resources such as minerals and petroleum fare better. Once a contraction starts, pharmaceuticals, foods and necessities are worth investigating. In the trough of a recession, equipment, transportation, and construction perform comparatively better. Towards the end of a recession financials come into their own. When the economy is back into an expansionary mode, consumer cyclicals such as cars, furniture, durables, and luxury items do better. Banks also fare better in expansions. Generally, companies that sell essentials such as food, movies, tobacco are less sensitive to economic cycles. Industries that buy expensive plant and have high fixed costs are also sensitive to cycles. This includes companies that are highly leveraged. While ETF's provide a way to invest in individual sectors, knowing when to predict the next leg of the cycle, and before anyone else does, requires some diligence.

The Market

Stock markets are largely about trading, and not just companies raising capital to grow their businesses. Prices are determined by the aggregate opinions of investors who base their decisions on expectations of future performance. Investors may also be basing their expectations on how they think other investors are likely to behave. Despite this, or because of it, the daily gyrations of prices often seem very random, and trying to guess which way markets will go from one day to the next can be frustrating. Investors often seem to be behaving irrationally. Sometimes they are right and make money, and other times the reverse is true. Is there a method to the madness? The stock market is forward looking and is a leading indicator of the direction of the economy. Each trade represents a view on the market. To trust whether the aggregate view is the correct one takes a leap of faith. Over the long term, markets don't display the same predictive track record as they do over the short term. For the buy-and-hold investor, then, markets do not offer a crystal ball. But they do offer a clear view into the past.

Historically, markets have always recovered. The last two stock market crashes took between eighteen months to two years to recover. From 2009 to 2020, markets have shown a resilience that has confounded expectations. The economy, on the other hand, has trundled along comfortably, but unremarkably. Despite unemployment reaching very low levels, wage growth has been largely stagnant. So how can markets outperform the economy? It is partly due to monetary policy, which has had unintended consequences such as the misallocation of capital. Companies have not been investing in productivity as was intended by central banks. Instead, many companies engaged in share buy-backs. This may reflect their uncertainty about the future and their own growth prospects. Share buy-backs push up share values. This rewards investors, but it also benefits managers who have stock options in their companies. They prefer buybacks over paying dividends, which reduce share values. This creates a conflict of interest. Managers argue share-buy backs are a good use of available funds, but others say profits should be put to better use, and that the practice only encourages speculation.

Shares offer better returns over the long-term than any other asset class. Bonds offer stability to a portfolio. All things being equal, investors should be able to invest with the knowledge that their retirement will be secure. However, heightened volatility creates a lot of uncertainty. Those dependent on their own resources for retirement face an evolving challenge that requires updating skills and knowledge to navigate the changing investment landscape. Being aware of the undercurrents which affect markets helps shape a view to better serve investing decisions.

Chapter 3

Behavior

Anyone who has placed a bid for an item on eBay will know how emotions can run high during the bidding process. The temptation to bid higher, often at the last moment, can be strong resulting in over-paying. Auctions are designed precisely with this in mind. A more rational approach is to avoid actively bidding by placing a maximum bid and allowing others to bid against it. This approach has a built-in safety mechanism that avoids irrational behavior, but not everyone uses it. Playing the stock market involves the same emotional responses for the unwary.

Human behavior is an important aspect of investing. We don't always act rationally and this is particularly evident where money is concerned, so it is important to understand why we act the way we do as it can help insulate against poor decisions that adversely affect performance. Behavioral sciences address issues concerning decision-making during times of excesses, turbulence, and crises. Asset bubbles have been around for a long time and are typically characterized by what is termed 'herd' behavior. Asset values are pushed to very high levels in a self-perpetuating upwards spiral. As values increase, so more investors pile in with the expectation that values will continue to increase. It is a form of blindness—or even madness—that causes investors to disregard the intrinsic value of an asset. Seeing that the herd is continuing to pile into an asset, the individual investor intuitively believes the masses must be right. When values reach levels that appear to be 'unsustainable', the so-called smart money withdraws. By the time the herd realizes what is happening, the downward spiral is already underway. A mass rush for the exit follows as the bubble bursts and asset values crash.

Another behavioral trait is risk aversion. We fear losing something more than being gratified by gaining something. We act irrationally when markets are volatile. Equally, we are over-confident when markets are doing well and tend to over-trade, attributing success to our own prowess. In the same manner, failure is chalked up to external factors beyond our control. Men suffer this affliction more than women. We also tend to respond differently depending on how something is described, or 'framed'. Something that is framed negatively, will elicit a different response than if it is framed positively. Most people would choose a half-full tank of gas over a half-empty one, because it is framed in a positive light. A 60% chance of stock price increasing if preferable to a 40% chance of a loss.

We don't understand probability. We would much rather have certainty now than gamble on having it in the future, even if the odds are the same and rewards greater. We also place more emphasis on events that have happened recently, especially if they appear in the media, a common source of the self-fulfilling, herd behavior. By assigning less importance to the future, investors don't save enough, or early enough for retirement. This has become a major problem with 60%

of Americans concerned they won't have enough money saved for retirement. Young people are susceptible to delaying contributions to a retirement plan, not realizing the significant increase in contributions they will need to make the later they leave it.

Trends steer investors towards predictive patterns of behavior, while ignoring the randomness of events. For example, a long run of increasing prices is taken as confirmation the trend will continue. While this holds true for some, for others the opposite is true. A continued trend must mean the trend will eventually reverse. In a probabilistic sense both are wrong. If a coin is tossed ten times and heads comes up each time, it doesn't make it more likely the next toss will be heads. It also doesn't mean tails is more likely. The odds remain the same: 50:50 heads, or tails.

Being aware of behavioral traits is a first step towards avoiding them. Self-awareness acts as a check on impulses and irrational choices. Understanding what motivates those choices reveals a side to them that may not be serving our best interests. The ability to stand back and question our own responses and of those around us can help guard against actions that ultimately lead to losses.

Investing Approaches and Styles

Top-down and bottom-up are two different approaches to portfolio construction. The top-down approach starts with asset allocation and then security selection. It starts with the general and fine tunes to the specifics. For example, top-down investors will look at the big picture such as interest rates and invest accordingly. If interest rates are low the focus may be, for example, on housing that benefits from low interest rates. While the approach benefits from diversification in a downturn, it loses during a rally by being under invested in growing sectors.

The bottom-up approach starts with the specific and works towards the general. It starts by seeking stocks that are under-valued. While this can lead to a portfolio being over-weight in certain stocks or sectors, it benefits from buying stocks that will have upside potential. Analysts of this approach look at individual attributes and product lines of companies and seek attractively priced shares based on ratios such as P/E (price to earnings) and financial strength, regardless of the macroeconomic conditions. One drawback of this approach is that there are often discrepancies regarding valuations, which are sometimes difficult to identify.

The two approaches are not mutually exclusive and many investors use both. Some will favor the top-down approach as the over-riding theme, but will fine-tune where the needs and opportunities arise to maximize risk-adjusted returns. Bottom-up investors will prefer to find value believing it the best way to hedge risk, but the goal will be to have a well-diversified portfolio that shares similarities to the top-down approach. The goal is the same, but the route taken is different.

Passive and active investing are two opposing styles of investing, already discussed in Chapter 1. Investing in passive index funds has grown in popularity since actively managed funds have failed to demonstrate superior performance when fees are subtracted. Other styles are growth and value investing. Growth seeks to grow a portfolio by sacrificing dividends that are then reinvested. Companies that have good management and products are expected to grow faster. Growth shares have a higher risk-reward ratio. Value investors seek stocks in established, larger companies that are undervalued believing this delivers better upside potential for growing a portfolio at the same time as paying a dependable dividend.

Although growth stocks may be more susceptible to volatility, value stock funds will be invested in the financial sector, which is susceptible to volatility in downturns. Passive index funds employ both styles to capture the benefits of both. There is no evidence that one style is better than the other. There is some evidence that value performs better over longer periods, but growth wins out over shorter periods. Generally, value stocks don't perform as poorly as growth stocks in a downturn or recession, whereas growth stocks shine when the economy is performing well.

Large cap and small cap are two more investing styles. Cap refers to capitalization and is a measure of a company's size based on its equity. Investors buy shares in large cap companies for their security as they tend to be established, large corporations. Small cap shares are more volatile, but outperform over the long term.

Combining cap size with growth or value is common. Small-cap value tends to outperform its small-cap growth over both the short and long term. However, when growth outperforms it is by a larger margin.

Evaluating Investments

Before buying anything, whether it is shares, bonds, funds, or real estate you need to know how well it has been performing. The two main performance indicators are based on historical income and growth, and the price you pay. The most basic and quickest method for determining price growth is by looking at a chart.

A linear chart that maps prices over time. To focus attention on the big picture, zoom out from a week, or month to five, ten or more years. You will see a different story emerges for each snap shot in time. Markets may appear in turmoil over short periods. When you zoom out to a decade or two, you may find markets have done well despite all the short-term volatility. Chart the boom-bust cycle years so see the speed of collapses in prices, and how long recoveries took. A note of caution when viewing charts over a period of several decades. Exponential increases over time may be compressed using a logarithmic scale. When looking at a chart this way, price changes can appear consistent. To get a better idea of the drama playing out look at charts that aren't using logarithmic scales.

The big picture is important for all buy-and-hold investors. Using charts is a fast and useful method to gain a
snap shot in time, or in determining trends. Using a
200-day moving average (DMA) smooths out the
bumps giving a clear picture of a trend. Linear regression does a similar thing, but it not widely used. Since
the mid-1990's, market prices have been more consistently and significantly above the linear regression
line only dipping briefly below it once during the
credit crisis of 2009. When the big picture points to
troubling trends, it is time to review your strategy and
evaluate exposure to high risk investments.

Evaluating funds doesn't require the same detailed
analysis as individual shares. You are buying into a
large pool of investments that is well diversified. Trying to evaluate each security would be time consuming, so the investor is more concerned with the sum of
all the parts. A simple method for evaluating funds is
to use a third-party ratings service such as Morningstar. The company offers two forms of rating; one
based on historical data, and the other looks to the
future using information such as management skill and
product lines. Morningstar's website also offers an
abundance of ratios and other financial data. Some
funds have reports written by analysts, that justify the
ratings given. Alternative investments are suggested
where analysts feel justified in so doing. Morningstar
is a subscription service, but a lot information on its
website is freely available.

When evaluating funds, investors need to pay attention to whether a fund is active or passive, and that

usually is determined by fees. Fees eat into performance. Index fund fees can be a fraction of one percent. Actively managed funds have comparatively higher fees, although that is changing as competition between active and passive have been heating up. Fees for some actively managed funds are now more competitive, offering the best of both worlds.

It is good discipline to dig a little deeper rather than taking professional ratings at face value. Having screened funds for good ratings, look at the funds graph which shows how a fund has gained in value. Compare the performance with another, similar fund, or its relevant index. Look at the fund's total return, which includes both dividends and growth. It will tell you how well the fund has performed compared to earlier years. You need to look back in annual intervals as far back as the data goes. Look for large, sudden fluctuations and determine whether they are easily explained by past events, such as recessions. Compare one year with the next and establish discernible trends. Was one bad year part of a trend, or was it an outlier?

The beta ratio is a useful measure. Beta is a measure of risk and sensitivity to the market. It tells you how well or poorly the fund performed against the index it tracks. A beta of more than one means the fund fluctuates up or down more than the index it tracks. The higher the beta is above one, the more the fund will fluctuate compared to the market. If beta is less than one, the fund won't gain or lose as much as the market when it goes up or down. So, if you were investing in a passive index fund that tracks the broad market you'd expect to see a beta of close to one. A portfolio with a beta of zero can be said to be risk free.

Alpha is the measure of how much a fund has performed in relation to the market. It is a measure of the excess return over a benchmark index and is more relevant, therefore, to actively managed funds. It is a measure of how well a fund manager is doing. An alpha of one means the manager has outperformed the benchmark by 1%. An alpha of minus one means a fund has underperformed by minus one percent. Outperforming the market usually means taking on more risk by selecting shares that are expected to do well. A fund with an alpha of zero would mean a manager is not beating his index and is not providing excess return. In this case, the investor needs to justify paying a fee. The information ratio is similar to the alpha ratio, but measures a manager's ability to beat his benchmark consistently. A low tracking error means the manager is consistently doing well.

The Sharpe ratio is another measure of excess return. It measures the return over and above the risk-free rate. The ratio has two parts; the excess return over the risk-free rate, and the standard deviation, which is a measure of risk. Risk measures the amount of volatility, or movement up and down of a share's price. The bigger the moves up or down, the higher the volatility, the greater the risk. The main value of the ratio is to inform investors they are being rewarded for taking on more risk than short term government bonds. A return less than the risk-free rate won't be acceptable to most investors. A positive Sharpe ratio is good, and the higher the better, although a ratio of one is considered healthy. A negative ratio would be a warning signal. A portfolio that seeks higher returns, usually is taking on more risk, so we would expect to see a higher Sharpe ratio. Like all measures that use assumptions there are drawbacks. Standard deviation doesn't account for un-usual events when volatility can be very high. There are also claims the ratio can be manipulated by fund managers. If the Sharpe ratio of an actively managed fund is the same as for the index it tracks, then man-agers are not beating the market. Generally, selecting a fund with a higher Sharpe ratio makes sense.

R^2 or R-Squared measures how much a fund's move-ment is explained by its benchmark. If a fund has an R-Squared of 100%, the fund's movements, up or down, are attributed to movements in its benchmark index. Anything above 85% means the fund moves closely to its benchmark. Less than 70% means the fund may be seeking greater returns and taking on more risk. If the R-Squared is indicating a close correlation to its index, but has a Beta of less than one, the fund may be offer-ing better risk-adjusted returns.

Standard deviation is a measure of risk. It calculates risk based on how far away something moves from its average. By looking at historical data we can calculate the probability of something happening. Standard de-viation measures risk based on the probability of oc-currences. However, it falls short of offering an accu-rate measure of all risks. In the last two decades to 2020, there have been three events that were outside the normal distribution: The dot.com bubble in 2000, the housing bubble in 2006, and Covid-19 in 2020. This limits the usefulness of standard deviation as it doesn't account for the frequency of outlier risks.

In conclusion, ratios are useful for measuring performance against benchmarks. This is especially so for actively managed funds that seek to outperform their benchmarks. Ratios are also useful for comparing funds with each other. Using them to predict future returns is of limited value as past performance is never a guarantee of future performance. For those investors determined to test their trading skills by buying individual shares, there are some key financial ratios worthy of consideration. These ratios are often freely available online, which takes the leg work out of rummaging through annual accounts for the relevant numbers.

Financial Ratios

Financial ratios look at the financial soundness, and profitability of a company. There are two main financial reports in a company's annual accounts; the balance sheet, which measures financial health, and the income statement, which measures profitability. The balance sheet is snap shot in time, whereas profitability represents the performance over annual, or shorter intervals. Some ratios use numbers taken from both the balance sheet and income statement. Given that they measure different time intervals, ratios can become distorted. A company's annual report includes written accounts from management describing the year's performance. The final published accounts are audited by an accountancy firm, which gives an opinion as to whether they believe the accounts accurately reflect a business's performance. This acts as a check on companies who may otherwise be tempted to massage numbers to promote themselves in a more favorable light to shareholders. Financial audits also prevent companies from deliberately covering up things that negatively impact their operations and reputations.

It is important to realize that annual financial reports suffer from a lag between year-end and publication. The information is, therefore, not always timely and puts investors at a disadvantage. Some companies do produce quarterly performance updates, so shareholders can monitor things on an on-going basis. Estimates of future earnings help investors with future expectations for growth and returns. Overly optimistic predictions of future growth need to be taken with a grain of salt.

The balance sheet is split between assets and liabilities. In other words, it presents what a company owns and what it owes. A healthy balance sheet is when a company owns more than it owes, ergo, its assets exceed its liabilities. What constitutes an asset or a liability can sometimes be confusing giving rise to concerns that some companies may overstate assets, or understate liabilities.

Investors also want to know that a company is profitable. After deducting all costs from revenues, the net proceeds are distributed to the shareholders. Accounting conventions are based on a system of accruals, which calculates amounts owed or owing, so does not necessarily reflect a true cash position. A certain element of 'opinion' is therefore attached to the profit number in annual accounts.

Performance ratios need to be viewed over a period of several years so comparisons can be made. Investors and analysts are looking for something that bucks the trend. It may be to confirm what they already suspect or know. Viewing a ratio in isolation may not paint the whole picture. If a company made a loss in one year, there may be a legitimate explanation. If losses have occurred over consecutive years—and are worsening—this will raise a red flag. Most of the numbers for perform common ratio calculations can be found in the annual accounts of companies. However, the following ratios are mostly readily available on the internet so don't need to be calculated.

Current Ratio
The current ratio measures short term (current) assets against short term liabilities. Short term assets include cash, inventory, and what a company is owed. Short term liabilities include what a company owes to its suppliers; its loans, and dividends due to shareholders. Investors and other parties want to know that a company has enough cash and assets that be converted to cash quickly to meet current liabilities. A ratio of one or greater is a healthy indication. Manufacturing businesses may have a ratio of two because of their larger inventory levels. It is assumed inventory

can easily be converted to cash. This may not always be the case, however.

Quick Ratio
The quick ratio is like the current ratio, but removes inventory, since it may not be easily converted into cash. It is assumed that accounts receivable—what a company is owed—is easily collectible. Normally, companies extend credit, which is a period in days that creditors allow companies to pay for their supplies. Companies that are buying supplies may also be selling to other companies and offering their own credit terms. Cash flow problems can arise when companies don't negotiate favorable credit terms. Companies that require payments upfront, such as retail, don't offer credit terms to customers so will benefit more from having credit terms with their suppliers. A ratio of one, or greater indicates a company can meet its short-term liabilities.

Debt to Equity Ratio
Companies need to raise money outside their operations to fund their longer-term business operations. They can do this by selling shares or issuing bonds. On a balance sheet, shares are represented by equity and bonds by debt. The higher the level of debt to equity the riskier the company. When interest rates are low and companies can borrow cheaply, they may be tempted to borrow more, thereby, increasing their debt levels. When interest rates rise, this can put pressure on debt repayments. Bond holders expect a consistent stream of income, which can put pressure on

over-leveraged companies to generate sufficient income to service bond obligations. This becomes especially important if revenues decline as economic and business conditions change. Typically, manufacturing, utility, and established companies with reliable income streams have higher level of debt to equity. A ratio of one indicates a company is equally dependent on both forms of raising capital. A ratio of two may be a sign too much debt is being taken on. A ratio in the range of 0.3 to 0.6 is acceptable. A higher debt to equity ratio may be caused by share buy-backs. I go into this in more detail about share buy-backs under the valuations section that follows.

Interest Cover
The interest cover ratio shows whether a company can cover its debt such as loans and bond payments with its profits. Is it making enough money after expenses to pay its obligations to bond holders and banks? Lenders and bond investors clearly have an interest in this, but so do shareholders who want to know that there will be enough profit after debt payments to pay dividends. The ratio shows whether a company is profitable, and whether its level of debt is high. The ratio is not perfect since it uses numbers from the income statement, which covers a year's activity, and the balance sheet, which is a snapshot in time. The higher the ratio is above one, the better. A ratio equal to, or below, one may mean a company is struggling to meet its debt obligations.

Return on Equity (ROE)
This ratio provides useful information to investors about how well a company is using shareholders' capital to generate profits. Since net profit is used in this ratio, a positive number denotes the company is profitable and able to provide a return to investors, even after the deduction of all other costs, such as interest payments and taxes. A good comparison is with the market, say the S&P 500, that has an average of about 13% return on equity. Utility companies will have a lower ratio due to bigger balance sheets and smaller profits. For technology companies, the reverse is true. Excessively high ratios are a warning sign and may be an indication of inconsistent profits, or the use of debt to buy back shares.

Return on Assets (ROA)
The return on assets ratio is like the return on equity ratio. It is a measure of how efficiently managers are using their assets to create profits. The ratio compares net income to total assets, including liabilities. This is useful since both debt and equity are used to generate growth. As with ROE, the ratio will differ by industry sector, so is only useful as a comparison with peer companies, or when comparing with previous years. The higher the ROE to ROA, the higher the level of debt. The higher the level of debt, the more risk a company assumes. A ratio of 5% may be considered a healthy return on assets.

Dividend Payout Ratio
This ratio tells investors the amount of profit that is being paid to investors as opposed to being ploughed

back into the company for growth. Younger companies will, therefore, have lower payout ratios since they still need to grow. More mature companies will payout a higher percentage of earnings to shareholders. Paying out more in dividends may point to slower future share price growth. This may be because a company has passed through its rapid growth stage. Investors will be looking for consistency in dividends, but may reason a very high payout ratio is not the best use of earnings and is not justified. The ratio varies depending on the business sector. Income-seeking investors will be looking for companies that pays out a third to half of their net earnings. REITs (Real Estate Investment Trust) and MLP's (Master Limited Partnerships) are exceptions to this rule of thumb, since they must pay out most of their profits.

Earnings per Share (EPS)
This is a commonly used ratio by investors, because it tells them how much profit is generated per share. It is calculated by dividing net profits by the total number of shares in a company. It is a measure of profitability. The higher the EPS, the greater the profit, the more willing investors will be to pay for the shares. There is no useful range that indicates a healthy EPS, but a positive number is encouraging. A common use of this ratio is in calculating the more widely quoted price-to earnings ratio, or P/E for short.

Price-to-Earnings (P/E)
The price to earnings ratio is often used as a yardstick for a share's comparative value. It also tells you roughly how many years it would take to recoup your

investment. It doesn't tell you much in isolation, but is useful when comparing with similar companies. It is calculated by dividing the price of a share by its earnings per share. If the price is high relative to earnings per share, it can make the shares look more valuable than they are. It may indicate a company has good prospects, but it could also mean investors are being overly optimistic. A low P/E ratio may indicate an undervalued stock, but it could also indicate a company that is underperforming. Another drawback of this measure of value is that earnings are calculated in different ways. A very high P/E could equally indicate problems ahead, or that investors are prepared to pay more for a company they are confident will do well. A high P/E may also be due to a large investment in production. Similarly, some companies exhibit lower earnings by the nature of their business. Another misreading resulting in a high P/E may be due to low interest rates that artificially inflate the value of shares. This is because interest rates have an inverse relationship to value.

Given some of the limitations of the P/E ratio, analysts also look at the PEG ratio (Price to Earnings to Growth ratio). As it names implies, it measures earnings growth, over a period of one to five years, and is considered by some an accurate estimation of valuation. A value of one signifies fair value, below one points to being undervalued, and above one indicates shares are overvalued. It is especially useful for companies that have high rates of growth and high valuations.

Z-score
A Z-score is a measure of a combination of key financial ratios and is used to determine the likelihood of bankruptcy, or financial health of a company. The score works by comparing data sets to peer group averages and uses standard deviation as the unit of measure. A score of 1.8 is means a company may be in serious difficulties and a score of 3 is considered safe. Since the Z-score depends on published financial data, it is only as good as that data. Struggling companies may be tempted to obscure their performances and financial health from public scrutiny. That said, the Z-score has a consistent record for providing accurate assessments.

Establishing value is important when buying anything whether it's food, cars, homes, art, or shares. For items that are produced we pay the cost of production plus the profit margin. However, for items such are art and financial assets things are not so clear cut. How does an investor know when shares are over-valued, under-valued, or fair value? If establishing value is important for most things, shouldn't it be so for financial investments? After all, we put more money into investments that just about anything else. Importantly, the more excessive valuations appear to be, the more important the need to establish some yardstick of intrinsic value.

When prices exceed normal expectations, it makes for a unforgiving investment environment. Very high valuations signal volatility, and are always followed by steep price declines. What goes up must come down. The higher prices go up, the further they have to fall.

How to navigate choppy waters presents a challenge even to the most experienced investors. So, we need to find a point of beginning. To have value, something must start with some tradeable worth. To say something is worth what somebody is prepared to pay for it doesn't provide us with a useful template. Since financial assets are not tangible products their value is allusive. So, their value to us is determined by what they can do for us, which is to provide growth and income. Another way to establish value is by measuring the tangible, or book value of a company in relation to the number of shares. However, none of these explains how values reach such excessive levels, and investors need to be leery of attempts to do so.

Fundamental Analysis

Fundamental analysis is concerned with finding the intrinsic value of a share, as opposed to its market value, or current price. The distinction is important since intrinsic value and market price can differ significantly. For example, if the intrinsic value of a share indicates a much lower value than the current market price, then the share is probably over-bought, in other words, over-valued. In the following paragraphs, I attempt to breakdown what we mean by intrinsic value and offer some tools for its calculation. Chapter 5 will explore the wider context of fundamental analysis vis-à-vis the economy.

Tobin's Q

A building blocks of a company's worth are its physical assets; equipment, buildings, plant etc. They will have a value, or replacement cost. The company will also have a market price, which the financial markets will place upon it. These two values will possibly, or even likely, be different. Tobin's Q is a ratio that measure this difference. A Tobin's Q of more than one means the company is considered a good bet as the market believes it has growth potential. It may also be that investors are overly optimistic. By the same token, a ratio of less than one could mean the company is under-valued, so possibly a bargain. A fair value is, therefore, equal to a ratio of one.

Value based on physical assets seems like a feasible way to assess a company's worth. However, there are different kinds of assets, some of which are not tangible, such as good will, or brand that are not factored into this ratio. Tobin's Q is useful as a measure of value for the market and is used by the Federal Reserve Bank in the US. Interestingly, the ratio, often referred to as the 'Q' ratio, has been consistently higher than one since the early 1990's. There have been brief periods when it has fallen below one, but these have been associated with sharp market declines. It peaked at a ratio of two twice in that period. From the early 1900's the ratio rarely exceeded one remaining for the most part below one.

CAPE (Cyclically-Adjusted Price-to-Earnings)

We've explored the difficulties of valuing shares, and the market. What about mutual funds and ETFs? Net

Asset Value (NAV) is a fund's total asset value less all its liabilities. When divided by the number of shares in the fund, it gives us the price at which the funds are traded. However, this doesn't tell us if the fund itself represents fair value. You could look at all the individual companies within a fund to compare P/E ratios with peer groups, but this would be very time consuming. Alternatively, if a fund tracks an index, the CAPE ratio (Cyclically-Adjusted Price-to-Earnings) offers a useful measure of value. It averages the EPS over a ten-year period smoothing out the bumps and adjusting them for inflation. The CAPE ratio was the result of research, which found share values move up and down much more than their underlying earnings.

The CAPE average for the market is 16.7 and as of May 2020 stood at 27.83. It reached its peak (44.19) prior to the dot.com bubble in 1999. Professor Robert Shiller, a co-creator of the ratio, has intimated that buying into the market when the ratio is above 20 is unlikely to offer the investor long term gains. That is to say, the market is over-valued. It is interesting to note that while the CAPE ratio clearly indicates that markets are over-valued, its more commonly used cousin the P/E ratio paints a different picture. The average P/E ratio is 15.78 and stood at 21.27 in May 2020. That is a 35% increase above the average, which is significant. The CAPE ratio, however, is 67% above its average for the same period. For comparison, the PEG for the S&P 500, which usually resides within the range of 1 to 1.5, breached the 2 level in 2020. It should be borne in mind, however, that the PEG is generally a better measure of individual stock valuations. It should be noted the CAPE ratio has been criticized for ignoring changes in accounting rules and share buybacks. Professor Shiller's website confirms the ratio now does at least adjusts for share buybacks.

Dividend Discount Model (DDM)
The dividend discount model, also known as the dividend valuation model (DVM), tries to determine the fair, or 'intrinsic' value of a stock by looking at the income it produces. If an investor wants a 5% return, which we call the RRR (Required Rate of Return), he multiplies the stock price by 5% plus growth. If the calculation gives a number greater than the current price of the stock, the current share price represents good value. The formula is:

$$\text{Expected Return} = \text{Dividend/Price} + \text{Growth}$$

DDM is only useful when analyzing mature, 'blue chip' companies that pay a consistent dividend. It should also be noted the calculation is very sensitive to inputs so can produce widely differing results. The calculation can be performed using a spreadsheet. There are also one or two online calculators available to use. Most of the data that you need to input can be found on the internet, but care needs to be taken as to the accuracy and reliability of sources. Methods, data and results can vary. Luckily, Morningstar produces a stock price valuation guide using a simple star system. One star means a stock is over-valued, three equals fair value and five stars represents under-valued. The guide also indicates whether the valuation is certain, or uncertain. Seeking confirmation of valuations from different sources is par for the course.

Price to Book Ratio (P/B)
The book value of a company is its assets minus liabilities (debt, loans, etc.) and intangibles items (good will, patents etc.). Examples of assets are equipment, buildings, cash, inventory, and accrued income. If you sold off, or liquidated a company's assets and paid off its debts, you would receive its book value. The ratio measures book value against the market value of a company's equity, which is usually higher. Equity value is a company's share price multiplied by the number of its shares, so its price is fixed by the market. A ratio of one is going to be attractive to value-seeking investors. If the ratio drops suddenly below this level, it could indicate financial distress. The ratio is less useful for companies operating in the services sector because they usually have fewer tangible assets. The P/B ratio is often looked at in conjunction with the ROE (return on equity). They should move more or less in lock-step, so when they diverge it can be a warning sign. If the REO is low but the P/B is high, it may signal shares are over-valued. It should be noted share buy-backs can distort the P/B ratio making it less useful as a measure of value.

In conclusion, financial ratios that examine balance sheets and income statements are only useful for investors who want to buy shares in individual companies. They try to determine the financial health and operational efficiency of a company. Since they use historical data, their usefulness in predicting future performance is limited. Investors who seek value as a strategy, believing that undervalued shares offer the best opportunity for upside potential will find value ratios useful. For buy-and-hold investors who seek to invest more broadly in either actively managed or passive index funds, ratios that examine fundamental analysis are useful. In addition, investors need to look at how well the fund performs in relation to its benchmark. This is especially important for actively managed funds, where the investor will be seeking positive alpha.

The broad market needs to be viewed against the backdrop of the economy, monetary and fiscal policy, interest rates, inflation, the business cycle, and other fundamentals that have a bearing on valuations. A major concern arises when markets become very overvalued. Ratios can indicate when this occurs both in the market in general, and at the company level, offering the value investor the opportunity to look for opportunities. Remember, investing in any assert class that offer value hedges against downside risk because it provides a cushion and upside potential.

Bond Fund Valuation

Bonds are more efficiently priced than equities. Bond prices move inversely to interest rates. Bond funds comprise many different bonds that are pooled so pricing, some will argue, is not possible or relevant.

Fair value is deemed to be the market price, and valuations are largely calculated using comparisons with similar investments. Other inputs to calculate price include interest rates, the yield curve, credit risk, default rates and volatility. There are no equivalent EPS, P/E, PEG, or CAPE ratios for Bond funds. However, Morningstar's average weighted value gives an indication of whether a bond fund is close to par value. This may offer some comfort over interest rate sensitivity.

iShares is a major leader in ETFs and has a price/yield calculator on their website. You can input either the desired yield to find the price you would need to pay, or vice versa. Well diversified bond funds typically lost value during the credit crisis for a short period before making up the lost ground. During the trough in late October 2008, yields were attractive offering around 5%, so investors were being rewarded adequately. This would seem to suggest prices were showing some susceptibility to volatility and not just interest rates. Since then, prices have moved steadily upwards pushing yields down to levels that are not so attractive to investors. The reason why investors still hold bonds and bond funds is for total return, which has been good. For fixed income investors, this isn't helpful since it entails realizing gains to substitute for income. With the current low interest rate environment and central bank monetary easing, it may take another severe shock to credit markets, or high inflation for bond funds to become attractive fixed income investments. Some analysts believe is could be many years before we a return to normalization in yields. The long term effects of this are not known, and pensions and insurance are negatively impacted.

In 2019, the Bank of Japan tried to correct this imbalance by encouraging yield to rise on bonds with long maturities, while keeping them low for short maturities. It should be remembered that Japan lowered rates to zero and started QE before anyone else. Neither seemed to stimulate the Japanese economy. Both the Bank of Japan and European central bank have introduced the highly controversial negative rates with little to show for it. The bond market is facing major challenges, and investors will want to proceed with caution when investing in it. Some investors may wish to avoid them altogether, until a clearer picture emerges. While they offer relative safety, low yields are so paltry to be unworthy of consideration.

Chapter 4

Real Estate

The word 'Real' was a legal term used to convey something immovable such as land, or structures that sat on land. It is no coincidence that the French word for real estate is 'immobilier'. In this chapter, I am going to be looking at residential real estate. It has become increasingly popular as an investment either as part of a balanced portfolio or as an alternative to financial investments. There Is no doubt home prices have appreciated in value quite considerably over recent decades. That culminated in a bubble in prices in 2006-07, which eventually burst leading to the credit crisis and Great Recession in 2008-09. While it was regarded by many as a localized problem effecting major urban areas, especially in the English-speaking world, it was much more widespread than many realized at the time stretching from Europe to Asia.

Backdrop

The common thread that seems to run through all over-priced real estate is the record low cost of borrowing, coupled with the perception that real estate offers a safe investment that performs well. This perception has been built on a growing aversion to risk in financial markets that have displayed high levels of volatility. First, there was the Dot.com crash in 2000-01. The aversion to risk was then reinforced in the credit crisis of 2008, when both share and home values crashed. While residential real estate values reached a trough in 2012, they recovered dramatically over a relatively short space of time. Investors still perceive real estate as being a good investment, and easier to understand than financial markets. However, institutional investors also saw huge opportunities following the crash. Foreclosed homes sold on the court house steps were comparatively underpriced and quickly snapped up rapidly pushing up prices. Real estate, however, carries significant risks that are often overlooked.

To combat historically high inflation in 1979, which stood at 13% in the US, short term rates, known as the fed funds rate were raised to 19%. Since then, the rate has been systematically reduced and stood at 0.1% in early 2020. The fed funds rate (LIBOR in the UK) is the rate at which the banks make short term loans to each other to fill any funding shortfalls. Funds are pooled by banks and held at the Federal Reserve Bank. The interbank lending rate is set by banks, and not by the Federal Reserve Bank. The Fed targets the short-term rate by what is called open market operations, which is essentially buying bonds. The buying of bonds became known as quantitative easing, or QE, and is referred to as monetary easing. When this happens, the Fed is said to be accommodative towards the economy and markets.

The Fed can simply 'print money' electronically with no resulting account deficit. This printing and buying of bonds ultimately puts money into the accounts of the sellers of those bonds, so more money becomes available in the economy for lending and so on. This increase in the supply of money, or liquidity, is designed to stimulate the economy as businesses invest in increased production, innovation, and growth. When the Fed buys lots of bonds, the supply of them is reduced and pushes up bond prices. When bond prices rise, their yield falls due to their inverse relationship.

The fed funds rate is a key rate that shapes lending by acting as a benchmark for many other interest rates. It directly influences banks' prime lending rate, which is the rate offered to clients that have good credit. The prime rate then acts as the base from which other loans, such as home, auto, and credit card are set. The Fed also influences mortgage rates. Lower mortgage rates push up home prices. As with bonds, there is an inverse relationship between mortgage rates and home prices, although it can appear less immediate and obvious. Lower borrowing rates stimulate demand for home purchases. This draws more buyers into the market who then compete for the same homes, pushing up prices.

Prices and Bubbles

From 1990 to 2020, US national home prices have increased 189%. Price increases have not been uniform with some states experiencing much higher rates of growth. For example, home prices in San Francisco increased 291% for the same period. On an inflation adjusted basis US home price increases have been about 40%, while real wage increases have scarcely moved. Yet, the 30-year mortgage rate has slipped from a peak of 10.24% in 1990, to a low of 3.23% in 2020, a decrease of 216%. Another factor that contributes to increasing prices is supply, referred to as inventory. Inventory measures the number of months it would take the current number of homes to sell given the rate of sales at the time. Approximately six months of inventory is thought to be the equilibrium point, where supply and demand functions normally.

Lack of publicly available information is a general problem with real estate. In academic circles, this imbalance is referred to as asymmetry. It is the idea that not everyone has access to the same information so may be at a disadvantage when making investing decisions. This feeds into the behaviorist's play book that people tend to follow the herd. If most people are doing something, then it is probably OK to do it as well. This behavior intensifies when prices increase rapidly. In the case of real estate, behavior contributed to the creation of the bubble in prices that eventually burst in 2006-07. The housing market had become a frenzy of bidding wars pushing up prices ever higher.

At the same time, buyers were being encouraged to borrow, even if they had low credit scores, with lenders turning a blind eye to qualifying criteria. Lenders were happy to lend to anyone since they had reduced the risk of defaulting mortgages by pooling good and bad risk into securities that were sold to investors.

These were known as mortgage backed securities (MBS). When prices became unsustainable, home owners defaulted on their mortgages and the securitized loans went bad, creating a crisis in credit markets. Banks became fearful about lending to each other as nobody knew who was holding these bad loans. Since banks provide liquidity to the system, the credit freeze ground the economy to a halt. We had entered a new era in which homes were being increasingly viewed for their investment potential. Homes were behaving like securities. Prices had become dislocated from the fundamentals of value. They were showing volatility, which continues to this day.

When home prices crashed after the housing bubble, governments and central banks targeted prices to prevent further declines. This was to slow down the damage being done to home owners, lenders, and the economy. Interest rates were compressed and fiscal stimulus added, which included generous tax credits for home buyers at both the state and federal level. Interestingly, the decline in home prices was not uniform. Some areas suffered much more than others. Las Vegas, Phoenix, and Miami were good examples where prices corrected significantly, whereas California, which has been at the epicenter of the crisis was spared some of the carnage. Hawaii, similarly seemed to show resilience although its market is both unique and opaque.

The crash in prices took four to five years to reach a bottom, which was sometime in 2012, but the story didn't end there. Undeterred, the market resumed its former pace of growth as institutional and private investors poured money into heavily discounted, foreclosed homes. Within a decade home prices were back to their peak levels. An unintended consequence of renewed rampant home price inflation is a somewhat distorted market. The property ladder lost its lower rungs as young buyers could no longer afford to buy a home—despite the very low mortgage rates. The problem was compounded by tighter lending requirements. Larger deposits needed to secure loans increased in line with home prices and young buyers struggled to save enough for deposits. Parents are often forced to sacrifice savings, or increase their own borrowings to help with deposits.

Despite a robust rebound in the housing market it is clear distortions have again been created. The distortions are primarily to do with affordability, but the housing market has become a victim of its own success. A cycle of escalating prices has been created. As prices climb, home owners are reluctant to sell. This depletes inventory putting further pressure on prices. Inventory has also been effected by a lack of new-builds. Builders blamed this on increased material costs and a shortage of labor. The upshot is homes are no longer affordable to vast swaths of young people. This has rocked the property ladder because move-up buyers depend on the successor generation to sell their starter homes. Likewise, retirees depend on robust household formations to downsize. Many simply don't know how to tap into the huge home equity gains creating further paralysis in the housing market.

Risks

Financial behaviorists claim investors are risk-averse. They respond more to the prospect of losses than they do to gains. This may in part help explain the comparative paralysis in housing market. A large build up in home equity creates the illusion of sustainable wealth. Home owners have become content to believe the wealth is palpable and secure and that, somehow, this time really is different. But we know from the last crisis home prices can be volatile, and are sensitive to interest rates. If we imagine an environment where interest rates rise, home values would decline. This doesn't just affect variable rate loans. The leading cause of defaults and foreclosures is negative equity. Refinancing is not possible in a rising rate environment, and fixed monthly payments must be serviced even when values declines. Borrowers then find themselves in the uncomfortable position of paying more for their homes than they are worth. The only escape is a strategic default, which many chose during the last housing crisis. What is relevant to one's own home is relevant to investment real estate, where is risk is compounded due to the use of leverage. Leverage magnifies gains, but it also magnifies losses. In fact, leveraged real estate is one of the riskiest investment classes precisely for that reason.

Investors who seek to build a portfolio of homes will invariably use finance as home purchases require significant capital outlay. The success of this form of investing depends on appreciation in home prices, and the ability to add value. Value is achieved either by re-modeling or acquiring a property at a favorable discount. Both are hard to achieve and require years of experience. The practice of flipping depends on being able to buy as a discount and adding value. It is a high risk strategy and often a gamble. The ongoing costs involved in maintaining a property and servicing debt are also over-looked by many investors. This can easily lead to negative cash flow making the investor dependent on price appreciation alone. Real estate has been molded almost out of recognizable shape by decades of elevated price increases and the low cost of borrowing. The perception that bricks and mortar offers sanctity is an illusion. A significant portion of home values are linked to financial markets through the cost of debt and commoditization. Like financial products, real estate is inherently risky.

Navigating all the obstacles of hands-on real estate investing is not going to suit the passive investor. For investors who primarily seeks a means of enhancing fixed income, a cash purchase is the safest route. It is a buy-and-hold strategy that will produce both reliable income and gains. This of course assumes the investor is following a value strategy. The main drawback to real estate investing is the large upfront capital commitment to an asset class that lacks both liquidity and diversification. It also requires basic financial skills such as cash flow analysis and the use of a spreadsheet. Without these basic skills, the investor is flying blind. All too often, investors in real estate assume they are receiving a positive cash flow, yet are making a loss. This happens because many of the less obvious costs are ignored. Large expenses occur throughout the life of a home. Items such as roofs, air conditioning, replacement of white goods, sidings, and fences all need replacing and can eradicate all the gains for the year. Vacancy periods, a softening rental market and inflation are also costs.

Investing in real estate entails analysis of the rental market. Are rents stable, increasing, or soft? What is the average void period when a home can be expected to sit empty? Fixed costs such as property management, association fees (HOAs), property tax and insurance all need to be adequately covered by rental income. Having comprehensive insurance cover is essential and many insurers offer landlord policies. Investors who wish to manage their own properties will need to be thoroughly familiar with local landlord and tenant laws. A reputable property manager is worth his or her weight in gold and removes an enormous weight off the mind of the investor.

Returns

As a rule of thumb, expect to budget 50% of rental income on expenses. This excludes any loan servicing costs. If your required rate of return is 5%, and you invest in a single-family home purchased for $100,000, you will need to generate a gross return of 10%. For every $100,000 invested you will be aiming for a monthly rent in the region of $800-$1,000.

Capitalization Rate

The net yield of a rental property is referred to as the capitalization rate, or cap rate. A healthy cap rate is 5-7%. This can be a useful guide in assessing whether a home is undervalued, or overvalued. Using comparative rents for similar properties you can calculate the price by multiplying the rent by the required rate of return, in this case 5-7%. For example, if a property produces an annual rent of $10,000 and has a purchase price of $100,000, the gross return will be 10%. A 10% gross return is the equivalent of a 5% cap rate. Remember, expenses on average are about 50% of revenues. Expenses will vary so this is only a guide. The calculations are as follows:

$10,000 annual rent / $100,000 purchase price x 100
= 10% gross return

10% gross return x 0.5 estimated costs
= 5% Cap Rate

If the home is listed at more than $100,000 then it is over-valued, and the investor won't be able to achieve their required rate of return. A home listed at less than $100,000 would be a better deal. Below is a cash flow analysis for appraising residential real estate investments.

Cash Flow Analysis

Listing Price	$110,000
Purchase Price	$97,000
Rehab Costs	$2,000
Closing Costs	$1,000
Total Invested	$100,000

Income

Monthly Rent	$1,000

Expenses

Property Tax	$877
HOA	$1,800
Management (8%)	$912
Vacancy (5%)	$600
Insurance	$1,000
Repairs (5%)	$570
Gross Expenses	$5,659

Debt Service	$0
Net Income	$5,741

Cap Rate	$5.74%

The above cash flow analysis is for illustration purposes only, but it shows the typical expenses investors can expect to produce an acceptable cap rate. The offer price can then be adjusted to arrive at an acceptable cap rate. The list-to-sales ratio might help to determine if there is wiggle room on price. If homes are selling 5-10% below list price there may be room to negotiate. You can also ask for closing cost to be paid by the seller. Your Realtor will be able to advise you on whether an offer is likely to be accepted. Always use a Realtor that has experience with investment properties, and give them a copy of your spreadsheet so they can appreciate your investment goals. They will have access to the MLS (multiple listing services) so can provide a lot of market data.

Property taxes, HOAs, and insurance costs will vary considerably. Management fees will be in the range of 8-10%, vacancy periods need to be no higher than 5% on average per annum, and budget anything from 5-10% for repairs depending on the age of the home. Ensure you reserve for repairs and let funds accrue. You may have no expenses one year and a huge outlay the following that can't be settled by a monthly net cash flow alone. There is no debt in the above example, so it is assumed that the home is purchased with cash. If a typical 30 year, mortgage with a 20% down payment was used the cap rate would hover a little above 1%. And that is with record low rates. This would make the investment very sensitive even to small adjustments in fixed costs, risking negative cash flow and insufficient funds to service the debt. Using leverage requires certainty over home price stability and growth.

A 10% gain in home price appreciation over two years is a healthy clip, but most of that gain would be wiped out by selling costs, which range between 8-10% of the selling price. Homes will often require money spending on them, such as painting, new carpets, and repairs to make them marketable. Those costs can range from a few hundred to several thousand dollars.

Keeping accurate records and maintaining a monthly cash flow analysis ensures the investor knows whether a home is producing a positive return. It requires the same discipline as booking keeping for a small business, whether it's for one property or twenty.

Selling

Getting a feel for home prices can be done by looking at comparable prices of homes that have sold recently in the neighborhood. A Realtor will be able to offer a better appraisal when the times comes to sell. Otherwise the investor will depend on publically available information online, the accuracy of which can vary from source to source. A useful exercise is to compare online home appreciation estimates with the Case Shiller Home Price Index. This index is limited to twenty major metropolitan areas but also produces a national index. The index is calculated using home resale prices. It does this by calculating the difference in price from when a home last sold to its latest resale price.

Using repeat sales data is more accurate than using average prices, which can become distorted when outliers occur. This happens when a small number of homes sell at the extremes of the price spectrum. For example, if a home sells for $1 million in an area of homes with mostly much lower values, the average will become somewhat skewed upwards. That can produce misleading information about price movements.

The median price is better than the average as it adjusts for outliers. While the median and average often track each other closely, a divergence between the two is cause for concern, often signaling there is a the average may not be representative.

Several online Realtor websites such as Redfin, Zillow, and Trulia offer home price estimates. When comparing online estimates for home values, always choose the more conservative number, unless there is reason to believe it is unrealistically low. Comparing online estimates against the direction of the Case Shiller Index acts a useful check. For example, if an online Realtor service shows a home has increased in value 10%, but the Case Shiller Index indicates a 5% increase, investors will need to look at actual comps, and for that you will need a Realtor. Alternatively, choosing the more conservative estimate can avoid costly mistakes.

There is a tendency for investors to over-estimate values of their homes, based on mere hearsay. It can be very disappointing to market a home in the belief it is worth 'x' amount, only to be told by a Realtor it is worth considerably less. All those dream-plans to retire early can very quickly evaporate. Investing in homes is for the long term and requires a lot of groundwork to ensure it will perform well as an investment. With due consideration given to all the factors such as price, rents, costs, condition, and the real estate cycle homes can be a good investment, and can offer diversification within a broader portfolio of financial assets. To rely on guestimates, a feel, and recent

performance of the market will lead to disappoint-
ment.

Here are a few other considerations when investing in real estate. Homes are a depreciating asset. That works to the investor's advantage from a tax perspective, but all those tax deferrals will come due when the property is sold. Capital gains tax is a fact of life, so before committing to another project, estimate your gains net of tax. Real estate is a fixed, tangible asset that requires maintenance. Keeping on top of maintenance makes for happier tenants and prevents small problems becoming big ones.

Property Management

Using property managers can add a layer of risk so careful vetting and monitoring is vital. Using established firms, or following recommendations for reputable managers is advisable. Below is a list of some of the questions to ask a property manager when deciding whether to use their services. Your Realtor may be able to recommend a reputable manager, but it's still a good idea to follow up with questions.

Vetting
How long have they been in business?
How many properties do they manage?
Do they manage any of their own properties?
Do they have liability insurance?
What is the current vacancy rate?

What has been the annual rent growth?
Is the current rental market soft or hard?
How do they advertise for tenants?
What is the management fee?
How much are new tenant lease fees?
How much are re-lease fees for existing tenants?
Are there any other fees, commissions?
Do they work with only licensed contractors?
Do they provide monthly statements?
Do they provide annual tax forms?
How do they deal with rent arrears and evictions?
What are local rent control laws?
How is maintenance managed?
Is there a 24 hour call number for tenant emergencies?
What background checks do they do on tenants?
Are they managing their own properties?

This list is by no means exhaustive, but reputable managers will have standard replies so can rattle them off. It is important that you feel comfortable with your property manager, so a face-to-face meeting will help with that. You are placing a lot of trust in someone you don't know to collect your rent and pass it on to you. You will need to let them know you monitor everything. Queries over monthly statements is one way to do that. At the end of each year assess the financial performance of your investment. Let the manager know if the performance doesn't meet your expectations. Although this may not be their fault, if they think you are not happy, it keeps them on their toes and working harder for you. Develop a good working relationship with them. Remember, they are the ones dealing with things when they go wrong. If you aren't happy with the service you receive, don't hesitate to change the manager. Just be sure beforehand of the contractual arrangement you have with them. Things to watch for are calls and emails not being returned, account anomalies such as inconsistent rents, late rents, regular maintenance charges, and long vacancy periods. The bottom line here is that you need to manage your property managers.

Diversification

For investors who fight shy of financial markets altogether and only want to invest in real estate for its perceived safety, they need to be aware of the inherent drawbacks. The most obvious is the lack of diversification. Investors are placing all their eggs in one basket. Given that no investment is immune to economic downturns, if home values fall there is no uncorrelated asset class to help mitigate the risk. Recessions create unemployment, which affects rents leading to evictions and costly legal fees. Lost rent will impact those dependent on it for fixed income. Diversification within real estate is possible and recommended. It helps mitigate these risks. However, a diversification strategy is realistically only possible with the help of reputable property managers, because it involves investing out of state and internationally.

Investing across state lines means getting exposure to different real estate markets. Some markets become saturated and over-bought while others offer better opportunities for growth. Geo-climate risk is now a very real fact of life. Do you want to invest in an area that is suffering from increasingly violent storms? Properties may be cheaper and rents offer a good return, but insurance costs may be prohibitive. Property taxes also vary from state to state. Again, home prices may be comparatively cheap, but that may be because property taxes are high. High taxes keep prices in check, but they are a fixed cost and can adversely impact cash flow. Choosing to pay at intervals rather than annually can help spread costs. Luckily, property taxes can be paid online in most if not all states. Be aware of income tax obligations for rental income and capital gains for states and countries you invest in. You will be required to file tax returns in most countries where you invest.

Investing internationally for the retail investor carries its own challenges. Language, laws, transparency, available information, local economies and currency are all potential hurdles. Choosing a country with a developed real estate and robust rental market is a primary consideration. For US investors, the English-speaking world offers several jurisdictions such as Canada, the UK, and Australia. Opening an overseas bank account into which rent proceeds are transferred has become more difficult in recent years as governments have clamped down on tax evasion. The Patriot Act enacted by President George Bush in 2001 has made it a requirement that foreign banks report US account holders to the IRS. Many banks decided not to comply so won't open accounts for US residents.

Currency risk is very real and can make a good investment into a bad one over-night. Currency markets are notoriously unpredictable and can impact returns for months or even years. From 2004 to 2008, GBP to USD was mostly in the range of $1.8 to $2. From then on it has slipped slowly back, and from 2017 has remained in the $1.2 range. Investing in the UK between 2004 and 2008 provided huge currency gains before eventually reversing to provide weaker returns due to a weaker GBP. In turn, the cost to invest in the UK was reduced making it an attractive proposition for foreign investors. When interest rates are lowered, it weakens a currency as money seeks better returns elsewhere. This happened in the US in early 2020, as the Fed reacted with stimulus to counter the economic effects of the pandemic. The dollar weakened which helped with exports, but it increases the costs of investing internationally.

The benefits of diversification across regions, countries and property classes offer clear benefits. Having a multi-property portfolio mitigates rent shortfall risk. Ten smaller cash-flowing properties will hedge against vacancies better than three larger properties. States with concentrated industrial sectors are vulnerable to downturns. For example, Hawaii and Las Vegas depend on tourism, which is the first to be affected during a downturn. Large cities offer robust rental markets, but rental returns can be lower as prices are often high. Rural areas may offer better returns, but have longer vacancy periods.

Selection

Lower priced homes generally offer a better rent to price ratio. This is because there is a larger pool of renters in this space. Higher priced homes may offer better rent security, but vacancy periods can be longer which may generate an opportunity cost. This is because of the lost return that could be achieved by spreading the investment over multiple properties for a higher overall monthly return. As with shares there is an optimized risk-adjusted return, a sweet spot, where price, rent and risk converge nicely. Finding properties that carry minimum risk while offering an acceptable return will ensure investments perform well. Buying value is key and keeping an eye on the property cycle may help find opportunities.

Market Indicators

There is a dearth of information on real estate compared to financial investments. The upside is that since real estate prices move more slowly than financial markets, investors have time to look for signs of distress that may indicate opportunities. After the residential real estate bubble in 2006-07, the market finally bottomed in 2012. Price corrections were uneven across the board, but some urban areas saw as much as 60% declines. Opportunities were snapped up as institutional investors piled in. The window was, nevertheless, long enough for retail investors to find properties that offered good returns.

Leading indicators for distressed markets are declining sales volumes, longer DOMs (days on market), widening spreads between list price and sales price, higher fall-through rates, and increasing rates of price reductions. Concurrent indicators include falling mortgage applications, loan defaults, and increasing inventory. Lagging indicators will be price declines and a spike in foreclosures.

As home sellers become anxious about falling prices many will put their homes on the market to realize equity gains. They will also be trying to avoid negative equity a leading cause of foreclosures. Buyers, sensing seller distress, will sit on the fence in anticipation of further price declines. Once a home has sat for a period of 90 days or more, sellers will start to reduce prices to entice buyers. The longer a home sits, the less desirable it becomes, as buyers begin to think there must be something wrong with it. Increasing fall-through rates happen when offers are withdrawn during contingency periods, or the buyer simply pulls out. This might be because of problems with loans, or problems with the home revealed during the inspection period. As pressure to reduce price increases, the spread between list and sales prices will widen. Sellers routinely ask for more than they know they can get, but by a small margin. A 95% list to sales ratio means the market is functioning normally. Further confirmation of distress shows up in the increased number listings with price reductions. If prices reductions comprise an increasing percentage of all listings, it indicates a buyer's market is emerging.

A home price index is lagging indicator, so will confirm rather than predict a distressed market. Falling prices will lead to defaults, many of which will become foreclosures. This creates a downward spiral which feeds on itself. While not typical of all real estate cycles, the above scenario is what investors wishing to enter the market will need to consider. Buying an investment that is priced at, or below, its intrinsic value, offers higher returns and greater protection from future declines. How do investors establish intrinsic value in real estate?

Valuation

The 2006-07 real estate bubble exhibited the same 'irrational exuberance' as equity markets during the dot.com bubble in 2000. There are though important difference between the two. Shares are liquid. That is, they trade freely on open exchanges, whereas homes are sold privately, which can take weeks to complete. This has implications for prices as the data feeds slowly through the system before they find a sure footing. Home values are also affected by supply, and like bonds, values are influenced by the cost of borrowing. Unlike bonds, home prices are anchored to fundamentals such are rents and incomes. Home buyers have limits on what they can afford based on how much they earn. However, the relationship between home price and wages has become distorted by extended financial repression and record low mortgage rates. A clear bond-like inverse relationship between interest rates and prices now afflicts real estate. This has also given rise to affordability issues.

Bond values are calculated using Net Present Value (NPV), a method that uses future streams of payments. Homes do have potential future streams of cash in the form of rents, but rents are not tied to a discount rate. They are tied to incomes. Rents can therefore be used to calculate intrinsic value since they can't exceed incomes. Renters can only pay what they can afford, which is set at a fixed percentage of what they earn. Where this relationship breaks down—as it has in recent years—is when home values increase beyond their intrinsic values. Investors have been squeezing renters to their limits to justify higher prices they paid for the investment properties. This is the reverse of value investing. Instead of adjusting prices to meet the required rate of return, investors adjust the rents. In some cases, rents are well in excess of the recommended 25-30% of renter incomes. This not only creates an unhealthy investment environment it also reduces the usefulness of rent for calculating intrinsic value.

Cash Flow Method
All things being equal, a method of finding the intrinsic value of a home is to use a cash flow analysis presented earlier in this chapter. This is done simply by adjusting the offer price until it produces the required rate of return. Investors can choose a rate based on what alternative investments offer. For example, if investment grade bonds are offering around 6%, and the risk-free rate is 2% you can pick a point anywhere

between the two. If a 5% is acceptable, a home with a current market price of $120,000 would need to sell at $115,000 to produce a 5% cap rate.

DDM (Dividend Discount Model)
Alternatively, the DDM (Dividend Discount Model) could be adapted to determine the required rate of return and intrinsic value of a real estate investment. The formula would be the same as in Chapter 3. You would have to substitute share value with the current market value or list price of the home. To calculate the dividend growth, you would enter monthly rentals over a period of years. The higher the rate of growth of rents the higher the discount rate, the lower the intrinsic value. A home valued at $120,000 with rental growth of 4%, and a discount rate of 5% produces an intrinsic value of around $115,000, which is $5,000 less than the market value. This is very close to the value arrived at using the cash flow analysis. It should be remembered the DDM was developed for equities, not real estate, so results may be unreliable.

GRM (Gross Rent Multiplier)
The GRM (Gross Rent Multiplier) is a ratio used in the real estate industry to estimate value. It is calculated by dividing market price by annual rent. For example, if a home is valued at $120,000 and produces an annual gross rent of $10,000, the GRM is $120,000 / $10,000 = 12. Having calculated the GRM, it can then be used to establish home values, simply by multiplying the ratio by the gross rent. The formula and worked example follows:

$$\text{Gross annual rent} \times \text{GRM} = \text{Home value}$$

$$\$8,000 \times 12 = \$96,000$$

But this doesn't help us in finding the intrinsic value unless it is assumed the annual rent satisfies our required rate of return. The GRM ratio, then, confirms the market value of a home, rather than giving us an intrinsic value. So, to find a useful GRM, we need to start with a required rate of return and work backwards.

Assuming a required rate of return of 10%, a home that cost us $120,000 and produces a gross annual rent of $10,000 gives a return of 8.33%, which falls below the 10% we need. If we divided 8.33 by 10 we arrive at a multiplier of 0.83. If we now multiply the purchase price of the home of $120,000 by 0.83 we arrive at $100,000, which is the intrinsic value of the home. In this way, we have calculated how much we are prepared to pay based on a required rate of return. And the required rate of return is based on what we can achieve by investing in alternative investments such as securities or other real estate.

The same numbers can also be used, in a different order, to tell us how much rent we need to achieve our required rate of return. This of course assumes we are happy with the current market price of our investment home. Using the same example above, if our current rent yields 8.33% and we require 10%, we divide 10 by 8.33, which equals 1.2. If we multiply $10,000 annual rent by 1.2 it gives us $12,000, which is the annual rent we now need to achieve a gross 10% return. These simple formulae are a useful method for assessing the viability of an investment. Problems start when markets become over-valued, and the required rate of return becomes compressed. Investors must then lower their expectations. Instead of a 5% net yield, you may have to accept a 4% net yield or even lower, whichever is equal to or higher than returns offered by alternatives.

Earnings Model
From the year 2000 to 2020, median wage growth has been about 4%. For the same period, national home prices have increased by 115% while inflation, as measured by CPI (consumer price index), has been running at a little under 2%. The median home price in the US in 2000, was circa $170,000. If we take the average wage and median home price in 2000 and compare it to 2018 we find home values have outpaced incomes by 18%. In 2000, the ratio of home prices to wages was 5.29, whereas in 2018 it was 6.24. This roughly equates to how many years it would to take to buy a home. National averages provide a useful macro view, but real estate is local. Finding value is often at the micro level. Using macro measures based on income acts as only a guide to help locate value.

From the 1977 to 2000, home prices have hovered closely around 3.25 times annual income. If your income was $50,000 per annum, you could afford a home costing $50,000 x 3.25 = $162,500. From 2001 to 2019, home prices to income averaged 4.12. This is an increase in the amount home owners pay for a home, relative to their income. This change is because mortgages became cheaper, declining from an average of 10.25% to 5.04% for the same periods above. A one percent decrease in a lending rate approximates a 10% increase in affordability. Homes have become more expensive relative to incomes, but the cost of borrowing has declined. To arrive at fair value, the investor would need to adjust the home price-to-income ratio for the decrease in lending rates. For the purposes of valuation, using a ratio of 3.25 to 3.5 is a crude but useful benchmark. Simply multiply the median income in your selected location by the benchmark to see if valuations conform to, or are dislocated from, the fundamentals.

Affordability Index
Regional differences in home prices in the US are considerable. In San Francisco, homes prices increased by 120% from 2012 to 2020. That is a staggering 15% a year. A similar picture emerges for Los Angeles. Cleveland and Chicago, however, scarcely recovered from the crash in 2006-07. The NAR (National Association of Realtors) produces a home affordability index, which measures whether incomes are sufficient to be able to afford a median priced home. A value of 100 means homes are just affordable. Above 100 means home prices are within the means of average income earners, and below 100 signifies homes are unaffordable. Most of the unaffordable homes are located in Californian cities. How is this useful to investors?

Areas that have seen surges in home values beyond the national average will attract speculative behavior pushing up values further. Finding value in these areas is a challenge and rental yields will be meagre. Where prices have become obviously excessive the investor would do well to proceed cautiously. During the crash of 2006-07, home prices plunged by as much as 60% in some cities. Home price declines pose capital risk, and losses are magnified if leverage is used. Seeking value, therefore, plays a crucial role in mitigating risk and is much easier to find where affordability is not so much of an issue. It also helps fixed income investors since rent yields will be higher in locations where homes and rents are affordable.

Investing directly in real estate hedges inflation to a degree and can be a good diversifier, but probably shouldn't be more than a 10% allocation to a portfolio dominated by financial assets. Real estate is not, strictly speaking, a passive investment even if it is fully managed. It does carry significant risks often over-looked by retail investors. Thankfully, there are other ways to invest in real estate, which are passive so re-move some of the angst of dealing with the day-to-day problems.

Alternatives

REITs
REIT's (Real Estate Investment Trusts), are an indirect method of investing in real estate. Like mutual funds, they pool capital and invest in real estate. They are also offered as ETFs. REIT's come in wide variety of

flavors covering all types of real estate and even mortgages. Some are specialized while others are diversified. This offers investors the opportunity to invest in parts of the real estate sector previously only available to large investors. The primary purpose of REITs is to provide income, so they are similar to bonds, but are traded like shares. This means they are liquid compared to investing directly in real estate. Their attraction for fixed income investors is they are required to pay out 90% of their net proceeds and have strict limits on what they can invest in. This regulatory scrutiny makes them relatively safe for investors. However, since they are traded on financial market they are correlated with financial markets. When markets move in one direction REITs tend to move with them. This reduces their ability to provide diversification in a portfolio.

REITs are also impacted by the economy. A growing economy is good for real estate as rental growth expands with it. Higher rates lead to higher mortgage rates that boost the demand for rentals. Booming economies increase retail and office space so commercial real estate benefits. However, REITs are interest rate sensitive so as economies overheat interest rates rise pushing up capital costs, which impacts real estate values negatively. This particularly affects over-leveraged properties who struggle with servicing the higher cost of debt. Higher costs reduce distributable income to investors. When interest rates are lowered cap rates become compressed due to increasing values, which means investors will sacrifice returns.

REITs have performed well and have even outperformed the S&P 500 for periods. Since they are fixed income products they offer alternatives to bonds or dividend shares. They are backed up by a tangible asset so retain some sense of safety. However, they are correlated to financial markets and only offer minimal diversification benefits. Investors should note that if they are broadly diversified, they may be already exposed to REITs within a non-REIT fund. They are taxed as ordinary income so may be better held in a tax efficient account. Mortgage REITs are different in that income is derived from lending and not rents. They will therefore behave in line with lending markets making them sensitive to interest rate changes. As with any investment, investors will want to see strong management and fiscal responsibility. A payout ratio of over 100% may be a warning signal.

DST (Delaware Statutory Trusts)
This form of investment is only open to accredited investors, and is often used to defer capital gains tax from the sale of real estate. This deferral is called a 1031 exchange, and requires careful planning and professional guidance. Accredited investors are individuals who can afford to lose their investment and who understand the risks. DST's are a form of fractional ownership in commercial real estate through private equity. They pay regular fixed income and offer an above average return. DSTs have fixed hold period, after which the real estate is liquidated to pay off any loans used to acquire the property. This happens before principal payments become due. Investors assume the loan in proportion to their holdings. Many

DST's secure loans of 50% and above of the value of the property.

DSTs are put together by sponsors, who locate and buy large commercial properties such as luxury apartment blocks, retail and industrial space, hotels, and care homes. They raise capital through private investors and borrow the rest on interest only terms from lenders. The property is sold for a profit some years later and all loans paid off. During the hold period, rental income is used to pay interest costs and investor distributions. The success of the investment is dependent on the property gaining enough in value to sell for a profit before debt payments balloon, which is when principal payments fall due on the debt. This clearly carries risk and the success of the venture is going to depend largely on the experience and the skill of the sponsor. There is only a limited secondary market for these products, so they carry liquidity risk. Therefore, choosing reputable sponsors with good track records is prudent. Minimum investment amounts for DSTs are $25,000, or $100,000 for 1031 exchanges.

Compared to REITs, DSTs have a lower correlation to financial markets so offer diversification benefits. Diversifying within DSTs is also possible and advisable. Some DSTs already hold a diversified portfolio of investments. For example, it is possible to invest in multiple retailers across a range of sectors and geo-geographical locations. Investors should check to ensure only investment grade retailers are included in the offering. To diversify across other real estate entails spreading funds across several offerings in different geographic locations.

There are some simple tips for vetting offerings. Expect cap rates for multi-family apartment blocks to be 5% upwards and retail to be a little higher at 6% upwards. Cash-on-cash returns, which excludes debt are in the region of 5-8%. A revenue stress test tells you whether income covers expenses. A ratio of 10% means income can drop by 10% before reaching a breakeven point. The lower the leverage the better, which is typically in the region of 50%. Debt coverage ratios need to be within the 1.25 to 1.5 range. LTV (loan to value) needs to be within the range of 50-60%. Be suspicious of pro forma estimates of rental growth numbers that seem unrealistic. Be aware of front end loads, and ongoing management fees. There is also a disposition fee at the end of the term. A good indicator is when a sponsor acquires a property for less than market value. This provides a cushion over the life of the investment and helps ensure a profitable sale. Selecting newer multifamily residential complexes outside areas with geo-climate risk makes sense. When the sponsor has co-investment interests, it means they are confident in the offering. Invest time in understanding which sectors within commercial real estate best fits your risk profile.

TIC (Tenants-in-Common)
TIC is a form of fractional ownership. The name of this form of investment is a little misleading. Tenants, as in tenants-in-common, refers to joint-owners as opposed to renters or leaseholders. Its use dates back to British

common law. The structure is similar to DSTs, but investors hold title and not shares, so have a tangible stake in a property. TICs are also used for 1031 exchanges to defer capital gains tax. As with all matters pertaining to tax, professional advice is essential prior to investing. Income and gains are distributed in proportion to ownership stakes, which can vary from investor to investor unlike DSTs, which have minimum investment requirements. Leverage in TICs in now less common since the credit crisis in 2008. This may be a good thing for investors who want to avoid leveraged investments.

The main advantage TICs have over DSTs is control of management decisions. Fractional, or syndicated owners retain control. However, this can be a disadvantage if disagreement occurs between investors as major decisions require unanimity. If agreement can't be reached, the courts can intervene and impose partitions, which allows for conflicts to be resolved. Failing that, the sale of the property may be the only recourse. DSTs, on the other hand, are entirely managed by a professional company with no investor input. Unlike DTSs, which have a fixed investment time line, TICs are ongoing so are a good long term fixed income investment. This may not suit investors who wish to realize gains for quick profits.

TIC investments are put together by sponsors, so the leg work is already done for investors. Some, but not all, TICs are placed inside an LLC (limited liability company), which offers some protection in case of bankruptcy. Different tax jurisdictions may treat property tax liability differently. The TIC structure can also be used for smaller investments among family or friends. Pooling funds allows smaller investors access to a wider range of real estate investments. If a mortgage is used, all owners will be liable to service the debt, even if one owner can't meet payments. A foreclosure would mean all owners could forfeit their interest. Choosing like-minded partners and having water-tight agreements is par for the course.

Triple Net Lease (NNN)
Triple Net Lease investments, often referred to as NNN, are as close as you can get to passive investing in deeded real estate. Triple net properties falls into the category of commercial real estate and gets its name from the three costs the tenant pays; property tax, insurance, and maintenance costs. There are also single and double net leases where tenants pay only one or two of the costs, respectively. Lease terms are fixed for multiples of five years, and rent increases are written into the terms of the lease. Tenants range from major retailers to government entities such as post offices. The higher than average rent yields and hands-off nature of these investments makes them attractive to investors seeking passive incomes.

This type of investment has come about because businesses, such as retailers, benefit from a favorable tax deductible for rent payments. This means they are happy to be tenants and not owners of the buildings where they conduct their business, despite having the burden of costs of ownership. The other advantage to businesses of being a tenant is that it gives them greater flexibility to relocate, without the burden of selling.

Triple Net Lease investments are generally only open to accredited investors, as they require significant capital outlay. Although smaller properties can be purchased, the scope for diversification is limited so care is needed to select only retailers with solid credit ratings and good prospects. Buildings that offer flexible use will attract a wider range of tenants than structures built for a specific purpose. The price of properties will reflect returns, so it is important to assess the underlying value of the property, its location, and an exit strategy.

Crowdfunding

The credit crisis of 2008-09, led to tighter lending standards, making it harder for some companies to raise capital to invest in projects. Crowdfunding grew out of this environment by connecting investors directly with businesses, which needed finance but couldn't obtain it through normal channels. By cutting out the middleman and using technology, costs and fees are minimized. The flexibility of the internet allows small investors access to a wide range of investments, with small minimum investment requirements.

There are crowdfunding companies that specialize in real estate. Fundrise is one such company. These companies raise capital through their online crowdfunding platform and invest in real estate projects. For example, the development of luxury apartments that will be sold on for a profit, or rented out to provide income. There are three potential sources of income; rents, interest, and gains. The returns can be attractive. Income is paid out to investors in proportion to their investment. This form of investment is comparable to REITs, but shares are not publicly traded so they are illiquid. There is no secondary market for them, so investors are committed for the duration.

Some companies offer a range of investment options that emphasize either income, growth, or a blend of the two. This form of investment is relatively recent so there are risks—as with all investments—given they are untested in all market conditions. However, the level of technological sophistication has developed at an impressive pace, and allows smaller investors to invest in areas previously unavailable to them.

Bricks and Mortar

Real estate is an established asset class, and sits comfortably within an investment portfolio with other asset classes. Within real estate we have explored the different ways to invest in it, including residential, commercial, directly, either as sole proprietor or fractional ownership, or indirectly through public and private equity. For the more hands-on investor, investing directly in real estate requires careful selection. As with financial investments, diversification and risk-reward remains relevant. The greater the diversification the lower the risk. The greater the return the greater the risk.

Multi-family homes offer diversification across multiple rent streams and generally they offer higher yields. Since they will attract renters on lower incomes, the risk of defaulting payments increases during economic downturns. A single-family home in the median or upper quartile price range may offer more secure rent, but yields will be smaller and diversification benefits lost. This is because a multi-family home generates multiple income sources, whereas a single-family home provides one source of income. Rural areas don't have a strong captive market for renters, whereas urban centers attract younger, transient workers who prefer to rent.

Entry level single family homes in or close to urban areas are a good choice. Splitting your investment into multiple, smaller, less expensive single family homes avoids being 'overweight' in one. In densely populated urban areas apartments will offer a good investment choice. Care needs to be taken that fixed costs, such as association fees (HOAs), property taxes, and other costs are not unrealistically high. The advantage of shared walls is that maintenance costs are lower. However, high valuations in many large cities have cut deeply into returns as rents haven't always risen at the same rate as home prices. This has meant many investors in cities are content to invest for gains alone. In many instances, these gains have been handsome, but investors are often enticed into buying late in the cycle with unrealistic expectations of future performance. A strategy using high LTVs (loan-to-value), where prices are unsustainable, exposes the investor to interest rate and capital risk. This is often over-looked by investors, who are unware of real estate cycles and external pressures.

Vacations rentals can offer attractive yields but are labor intensive and seasonal so exposed to downturns and uneven income streams. The hospitality and tourist industries are the first to suffer when economies slow down. Student accommodation is an attractive investment since rents are not dependent on the availability of work and leases are often underwritten by parents acting as guarantors for rent payments. The properties are often fully managed so are attractive to the passive investor. Notwithstanding their appeal, of late there has been excessive supply of purpose-built offerings, based on overly optimistic student growth projections. The growth area has been largely in the foreign student market. The growing cost of education in some countries has caused students to look elsewhere for cheaper alternatives. This will impact purpose built accommodation where there have been clear overbuilding.

For those unfazed by sharing their home with a stranger, this can be a great source of income. A spare room can be a good income generator. Buying a home with a rentable space is also a good investment for supplementing income. Tenant behavior is better when the landlord lives in such close proximity. The mice never play when the cat is never away. Other secure sources of rental income are from governments, farmers and utility companies. Buying a hotel room may offer attractive passive income, but investors need to be wary of pro forma yields, which may be unrealistic. One or two companies are offering fractional ownership of single family homes. This offers great diversification opportunities, but investors need to understand the structure of the investment.

In conclusion, real estate offers the investor solid returns, comparable to financial markets, although over the long-term stocks have performed better. Since homes require a large capital outlay, diversification benefits are more difficult to achieve, especially for the smaller investor. Using leverage to invest in real estate increases risk significantly, as rents will need to cover the cost of capital in addition to normal running costs. Monthly monitoring of income and expenses using a ledger or spreadsheet, and budgeting for vacancy periods and large capital expenses is essential. Depending on home price appreciation requires knowledge of the dynamics of real estate. Avoid buying into over-bought markets. Markets are opaque and information is asymmetric so don't assume markets always have positive momentum and are trending in the desired direction. Avoid behavior that is shaped by sentiment. Let the numbers alone guide investing decisions.

Boom-bust cycles are now a common feature of the real estate market, characterized by excessive speculative bets, with increased volatility and potentially high drawdowns. Buying into over-valued markets will compress cap rates and impair upside growth potential. Default risk increases where leverage is used and price stability is low. Avoid the herd and suppress over-confidence built on perceived past financial successes. There is a tendency to attribute successes to our own skills and to blame external forces for our own failures. The complete reverse is usually the case. For the most part, increased home equity in recent years has been fortuitous and not owing to financial prowess. Likewise, failures are often caused by poor decisions. It is important to be aware of investor behavior such as risk aversion, regret and the disposition effect. Risk aversion places a disproportionate importance on losses than gains. Regret is when investors are afraid of making a decision so delay making it. The disposition effect is the tendency to sell assets with gains, but hold onto assets with losses.

Chapter 5

Technical Analysis

The role of technical analysis is to observe trends and measure sentiment in financial markets. It draws on historical data of prices and volume to help predict future movements that may offer trading opportunities. A continued trend is referred to as momentum. The strength of momentum is often given relative to the market. A multitude of technical charts exist that juxtapose actual movements in data against moving averages of varying length measured in days. By stripping out noise and varying the number of days used, different trends emerge. Infection points are created as moving-average lines cross each other and price lines. These inflection points may indicate buy, hold, or sell actions.

Moving Day Averages
Moving averages are used extensively in technical analysis. The idea is that averaging eliminates much of the noise of trading so more clearly identifies trends. The averaging is calculated by rolling the average forward over given fixed periods, for example 20, 50, or 200 days. This has the effect of averaging the preceding averages. If prices move below a 20-day moving average, it may indicate a downturn. If prices move below a 200-day moving average, it could mean a correction, or bear market. The S&P 500 crossed below the 200-day moving average in the years 2000 and

2008, both of which led to bear markets or corrections so severe that it took 18 months to two years to bottom out.

In February 2020, the S&P 500 passed below the 200-day moving average, but markets recovered quickly. Although there was a correction in prices, it was not sustained as markets appeared to brush off the concerns over the pandemic, Covid-19. Many analysts and investors were left scratching their heads, believing the massive stimulus packages from central banks and governments, enacted with lightning speed, was the primary driver for the price recovery. Nevertheless, investors used the inflection point to reduce exposure. As each major moving-day-average is breached, so more stocks are sold. Care needs to be taken that when prices cross a moving average, it isn't sudden because it could just as easily and quickly reverse directions. Moves need to be consistent and supported by a commensurate volume of shares being bought and sold.

MACD (Moving Average Convergence Divergence)
Traders will often use two or more moving averages together on one chart. When these two moving averages cross each other, or converge, it indicates a warning. When they stay apart, or diverge, things are safer. MACD combines the 26-day and 12-day moving average into one line called the MACD line, and charts it against the 9-day moving average. When the MACD line goes up it means divergence, and when it goes down it points to convergence so raises a red flag. When the 9-day line crosses above the MACD line, it

may be time to consider selling, and when it passes below it may be a signal to buy. A histogram, or bar chart accompanies the MACD moving averages. When the bars are tall it is confirmation of a trend, and when they are short it heralds a change. If the bars are above the baseline it signals a buy, and when they are below the reverse holds sway. The zero line straddled by the histogram indicates when the 12-day and 26-day moving average cross each other. When the MACD crosses above the zero line, the indicator is bullish, and vice versa. MACD is used widely by technical analysts.

Momentum and RSI (Relative Strength Index)
Momentum refers to the rate of change indicating whether prices are accelerating. This implies investors are bullish. Deceleration is evidence investors are bearish. It is a useful tool for identifying if a trend is ending. When momentum is flat, prices may still be going up or down but not at an increasing, or decreasing rate. A buy signal can be inferred when the momentum line crosses above zero, and conversely a sell signal is when the line drops below zero. RSI (Relative Strength Index) is another momentum measure, that is more sensitive to changes. When the line reaches 70% it signals a security is over-bought, which is similar to saying it is over-valued. When the RSI line drops to 30% or below it communicates the security is over-sold, so is potentially a buy signal. However, care needs to be taken—as with all technical analysis—since indicators are a guide and not hard and fast rules by which to trade.

Volatility and Bollinger Bands
Volatility measures how much a price moves so points to riskiness. If a price moves a lot, things become riskier. If it remains flat the risk lessens. Trading when volatility is low makes more sense that trying to navigate a market where prices are unsettled and moving in leaps and bounds. Bollinger Bands uses two lines that converge, or diverge from each other. When the two lines converge, that is they move towards each other, it may signal a breakout or sudden change in price direction either up or down.

Technical analysis tools are used mostly by analysts and traders. They have limited scope for helping buy-and-hold investors who invest in funds. They rely on past data, which is never a guarantee of future performance. However, understanding what drives sentiment and how trends materialize is useful to all investors. Moving averages strip out a lot of the noise so help discern trends, not just in individual shares, but also in funds. Technical analysis is useful in alerting investors to short-term indicators. Used in conjunction with fundamental analysis, it can also hint or confirm longer term trends.

Sentiment

Put-Call Ratio
The Put-Call ratio is a bull/bear sentiment indicator that alerts the investor about how other investors are behaving, especially during a market ruckus. Puts and

calls refer to 'options', which belong to the derivatives family of asset classes. A 'put' is an insurance policy that follows a pessimistic view of the market, and a 'call' is used to profit when markets are optimistic. When there are more puts than calls being traded, indicated by a ratio of greater than one, it is a sign markets are in risk-averse mode. The ratio may also be a signal to some investors who seek value. When fear grips markets prices tend to fall so can provide opportunities to buy shares at lower values. The ratio can be found on the Chicago Board Options Exchange (CBOE).

VIX Index
The VIX is a fear index produced by the CBOE that tracks options on the S&P 500 so is a widely used and relevant measure. It attempts to predict volatility, or risk over the near term. Remember, risk is measured by how much a price moves away from historical averages. It is referred to as standard deviation, or variance. When the VIX ratio is greater than 30 it indicates heightened volatility and when is it below 20, it represents greater stability. The VIX index moves inversely to the broad market, but in a more exaggerated way. As such, it can be traded and used as a hedge against market declines. Investing directly in volatility is not a long-term trade as the VIX index can reverse quickly. As such, this area of investing wouldn't normally be part of a retails investors portfolio. Derivatives such as options and futures are complex financial instruments and difficult to understand. If you don't understand it, don't invest in it. However, keeping an eye on volatility is something all investors need to do.

The Advance-Decline (A/D) Line
The Advance-Decline (A/D) line is yet another sentiment measure that reflects how much active investors
are either buying or selling shares. It is measured
against the direction of indexes. If an index moves up,
but the A/D line moves down it may indicate the end
of a rally, since fewer investors are active, or participat-
ing. If an index in is a downward trend, and the A/D
line is moving up it may indicate the market is about
to reverse course. If the A/D line tracks or moves in
parallel to the index it merely reaffirms the trend either
up or down.

So how does the investor act on these indictors? One
method is to reduce exposure by selling a portion of
holdings. While this won't prevent losses altogether, it
reduces the overall amount of loss. Have a clear plan
for scaling back by a given percentage per decline
rate. As markets fall 10%, you scale back 10% or whatever percentage you feel comfortable with. It is analo-
gous to dollar cost averaging but in reverse. In other
words, you divest out a market position incrementally
smoothing out many of the ups and downs. The use of
stop losses would be another method for reducing exposure. Stop losses are applied on trading platforms
when you sell a holding and are conditional upon a
price threshold or percentage decline being reached.
The sell order is triggered automatically so the investor doesn't need to be glued to a computer screen.

Fundamental Analysis

Fundamental analysis seeks to find the intrinsic value of a stock. The DDM (Dividend Discount Model) and financial ratios we looked at in Chapter 3 are part of this analysis. Since companies operate within the wider economy, it is also important to examine economic factors that may influence intrinsic value. Understanding the dynamics of the economy and how investments are influenced by it, will arm the investor with a broader perspective for making better informed decisions.

The economy goes through cycles of expansion and contraction. When an economy expands or contracts share prices generally move with it. As the economy grows bigger companies are more profitable so a greater portion of earnings are available to shareholders. If shareholders expect the company will do well in the future, share values will increase. The reverse is also true. In an economic downturn share prices may drop, often precipitously in a severe recession. By the same token, large moves in financial markets can impact the economy. If investors feel poorer because of declines in the value of their holdings, they will be less inclined to spend. When interest rates are raised to combat an over-heated economy, it becomes more expensive for firms to borrow so they invest less in plant and production. Higher interest rates also put pressure on home prices as mortgage rates will increase making homes less affordable.

GDP (Gross Domestic Product)
The key measure for an economy is GDP (gross domestic product). This measures how big an economy is, by calculating how much consumers and governments spend, how much firms invest and how much a country exports as opposed to imports. If GDP contracts it means the economy is contracting, which could lead to a recession impacting investments negatively. Share prices often move lower before a change in GDP so can be a leading indicator of the economy's direction. A note of caution is warranted as share prices often become dislocated from the economy. A case in point was in March of 2020, when share prices collapsed as Covid-19 gripped the world. The recovery in values was rapid despite growing concerns among economists that a severe recession was likely.

CPI (Core Price Index)
Inflation is a major factor to consider when investing. Inflation is a measure of how much the cost of goods and service has increased. The most common inflation indicator is CPI (Consumer Price Index), which tallies a range of commonly bought consumer items. At the other end of the spectrum is deflation, which makes governments more nervous as the economic consequences of falling prices creates a dangerous downward spiral. Investors need to try and anticipate what governments might do to combat inflation. The weapon of choice is interest rates. When inflation reached double digits in the 1980's, interest rates became very high causing a recession. Rates then followed a long downward trend to stimulate the economy out of recession, and in so doing, created what

many believed was the housing bubble in 2006-07. The cost to borrow became so low, it pushed up prices to excessive levels. Homes were behaving more like bonds with values showing signs of having an inverse relationship to interest rates.

Economic Theory

Underpinning government economic policy is economic theory. Two economic theories are prevalent in today's modern economies; supply-side and demand side economics. They are important to understand as they offer an insight into how a government might react to changing economic conditions. This is turn affects investment decisions for both corporations and individuals.

Supply-side economics imagines a well-oiled clock-like mechanism where the forces of supply and demand interact and adjust to bring about an equilibrium. This is where prices remain stable and everything is kept in check. Companies hire people who earn wages, which are ploughed back into the economy. If supply exceeds demand, prices fall until demand forces them back up again. Demand is never lacking because it is created by companies when they hire employees who then become consumers. The economy is, therefore, efficient and self-correcting. Ronald Reagan, Margaret Thatcher and Alan Greenspan are often associated with supply-side economics. Government interference in market forces was touted as being disruptive and by 'rolling back the state', businesses were free to operate unfettered by regulations and government over-reach.

Demand-side economists point out that markets are not smooth running mechanisms, because there are so many variables businesses must navigate, and this creates uncertainty. Uncertainty is not conducive to businesses investing and growing. Moreover, severe recessions with high unemployment would seem to indicate economies are not quite so self-regulating as supply-side economist would lead us to believe. The credit crisis in 2008-09 is often given as an example of markets not being efficient. Interestingly, it led Alan Greenspan, a former chairman of the Federal Reserve Bank to admit he'd made a "mistake" in assuming markets were self-regulating.

The British economist John Maynard Keynes, the father of demand-side economics introduced the idea that people don't always act in a rational way, often giving way to emotions and flights of fancy. Keynes conceived of the term 'animal spirits' that conveys the idea of the blind pursuit of self-interest. He further claimed uncertainty makes predictions in investing virtually impossible, and wild fluctuations in financial markets were a direct consequence of these animal spirits. It didn't matter how low interest rates were if there was doubt in people's minds about the future. Keynes believed that uncertainty played such a big role in decision making, it created what he called the 'liquidity trap'. It doesn't matter how much governments are central banks try to stimulate the economy, everyone will keep their savings liquid (in cash). Banks won't lend and savers won't invest. This is what contributed to the credit crisis in 2008. The well-oiled machine nearly ground to a halt, leaving many economists and investors bewildered, questioning their strongly held belief that unregulated, free markets can't be wrong.

From an investment perspective, losses were so great a distrust of banks and financial market became entrenched leading to social upheavals. Disparities is wealth came sharply into focus as banks and Wall Street, both often blamed for the housing crisis, seemed to have operated with impunity. The notion of 'moral hazard' emerged out of the ashes. It is the idea that governments will never punish for reckless behavior since the costs would be too high. Bailing out large companies and adding stimulus to the economy only rewards the behavior so ensuring its continuance. It is against that backdrop that investors had to contend.

The idea of animal spirits was further explored by Professor Robert Shiller who coined the term 'irrational exuberance' to describe investor behavior. He pointed to the disparity between movements in company earnings and wild fluctuations in share prices. While companies may have good, moderate and bad years, the underlying shares can move disproportionately higher or lower despite earnings. This reinforced the idea of a clear dislocation between share price and company performance, one that was mirrored by a similar dislocation between stock markets and economies. A dislocation over which economist became increasingly concerned in March 2020, following the pandemic, Covid-19.

Leading Economic Indicators (LEIs)
LEI's produced by the Conference Board combines ten different factors to show whether an economy is heading towards negative, or positive territory. Included are numbers on manufacturing, employment, housing, stocks, consumer sentiment and the yield curve. The yield curve is one of the most reliable indicators of a recession. When yields on a ten-year government bond are lower than a two-year government bond, it means investors anticipate a slowing economy, which usually ushers in a lowering of rates. This pushes investors into longer maturity bonds, pushing up their prices and forcing their yields down. When long term rates go below short term rates, the yield curve inverts, and a recession is likely to happen in the not-too-distant future.

Notwithstanding the reaction of markets to events in 2020, the yield curve had already inverted in August, 2019. A recession was on the cards before the onset of the pandemic. It is possible the pandemic triggered a downturn that had deeper structural causes, but its immediate impact on businesses and employment is not in dispute. It had caused a rapid descent into negative growth, and the V-shaped recovery many were predicting wasn't emerging. Investors response was bifurcated. Opinions were divided between those who thought markets were ahead of themselves, and those who believed markets were functioning as they should. The consensus, nevertheless, was that the full story had yet to unfold as the pandemic infection rate continued unabated. What is clear from this episode is that markets have a baffling and worrying propensity to confound expectations.

Both inflation and interest rates are key factors that investors need to watch. Expectations for higher inflation drive investors towards stocks and away from bonds. Inflation nibbles away at bond values, whereas stocks generally hedge against it. Bond yields benefit from higher rates, but their value is eroded when rates rise. Home prices benefit from low borrowing rates, which can be reversed when mortgage rates increase.

Exchange rates also impact investing. When one currency falls against another, inflation is imported as higher costs are passed onto consumers. By the same token, a weaker currency promotes exports since it is cheaper for other countries to buy exported goods. Countries which are net exporters, meaning they export more than they import, will benefit from having a weaker currency, and this will be beneficial to share prices especially for exporting companies. Exchange rates are connected to interest rates. High interest rates attract investment from other countries. As money flows into a country, buying its currency, the exchange rate is pushed up. Conversely, lower rates keep the exchange rate lower boosting exports and encouraging borrowing, which all help to boost a floundering economy.

With currencies floating freely on exchanges, a huge speculative market has evolved, driven in large part by derivatives that are used to hedge the volatile nature of exchange rates. For investors looking to diversify more broadly to include international exposure, exchange rates will add another layer of risk. There are many international funds from the broad to the specialized, and from emerging to developed countries, many of which hedge against currency risk using derivatives. I go into more details on international investing a little later.

Protective Put

A protective put is an option and falls under the category of derivative. Derivatives are financial instruments that derive their value from an underlying asset. It gives investors the opportunity to invest in an asset without holding the asset. Common derivatives are options, futures, swaps and securitized products. Derivatives are complex and will not usually form part of the retail investors portfolio. Options are split into two categories, the call and the put. The put option can be used for hedging risk as it acts a bit like an insurance policy. Another comparison can be made with a stop loss trade, which places a limit below which a sell order is triggered. The put option also places a price limit, known as the strike price, below which an underlying asset such as a share, or fund will be sold. The difference between a stop loss and put option is that the latter gives the option, or right to sell at the price, but not the obligation to do so. Like all insurance, you pay a premium which is calculated based on several risk-related variables. Unlike insurance, puts are for short durations so will be used when investors are certain of price moves over the short term. There are long term puts, called LEAPS that extend to 2.5 years. Unfortunately, there is no LEAP for the S&P 500 that allows investors to exercise the put before it expires. This LEAP put option has to run its course.

Selecting the correct strike price is important. A strike price below the price of the underlying asset makes more sense as it will be cheaper. This is known as an 'out-the-money' put since no benefit accrues until that price is reached, or breached. If the underlying asset doesn't decline in value, the put will expire and all you have lost is the premium you paid for the put. If the share value has increased considerably then the cost of the premium is covered. When a put is bought together with an investment, exercising the put triggers the sale of the asset. The investor is placing a floor below which he, or she no longer wants to hold an asset. If the asset value declines below that floor, the investor can sell at the chosen price.

Protective puts are used during times of market uncertainty, and high volatility. They are usually exercised a month before expiration. Choosing a put with a small bid to ask spread makes sense, since it will be more liquid thus easier to sell. Choosing an option with high open interest also means better liquidity. Delta measures an option's change in value relative to the underlying asset. For 'out-the-money' puts a delta of 30-40 is normal. Investors can expect to pay 1-2% of the portfolio value for the put.

Put contracts are in denominations of 100. To calculate the value covered by puts, multiply the strike price by

100. A strike price of $50 x 100 = $5,000 of asset covered. If an investor is protecting an index fund, the number of contracts needed is calculated by dividing the portfolio value by the index value, divided by 100. For example, a portfolio valued at $250,000 divided by an index value of 250, divided by 100 = 10. So, ten put contracts are needed. As with all investments, understanding value is important. The CBOE offers information on options, such as open interest and interest rates that can be used in online options calculators. Fair value is synonymous with the calculated 'theoretical value'.

It is recommended that investors become thoroughly acquainted with how options work before using them. A simple stop loss can be an effective measure against uncertainty and doesn't charge a premium. Futures serve a similar function to options and don't charge a premium, but are beyond the scope of this book. Inverse funds use derivatives to hedge against downturns and volatility so may provide a simpler alternative since the work is already done for the investor. A simpler, yet effective hedge against fluctuations in value of any asset is to buy when prices are low. The ultimate hedge for downturns is to hold assets in cash.

International Investing

Investing in other countries offers diversification benefits. Those benefits are derived from countries that have low correlations to the home country and high

Sharpe ratios (risk-adjusted return). Investing internationally carries risks inherent within individual countries. Corruption, political stability, foreign debt, exports, currency, inflation, current accounts, transparency, and GDP are a few of the important risks to consider. Developed economies may have higher correlations to each other than emerging economies, while the latter may carry greater risk. At the time of writing, while Italy had the lowest correlation to the US, it had a low Sharpe ratio, whereas Denmark had a slightly higher correlation and higher Sharpe ratio. Switzerland offered the highest Sharpe ratio among developed economies, but was more closely correlated to the US. So, the best risk adjusted return for US investors would favor Denmark. If reducing risk were the priority, more exposure to Switzerland would make sense. Few emerging economies were offering any diversification benefits during this period. While correlations were low, Sharpe ratios were mostly negative. It should be noted, however, that some emerging economies may have lower standard deviations than some developed economies. A general observation to note is that as markets have become more global, they have become more closely correlated.

Another measure of risk for international investors is a country's beta, which indicates how much it moves relative to a world benchmark. Finding betas for individual countries can be a challenge, but some results can be found on finance websites such as Seekingalpha.com. The higher the beta the greater the risk. A beta of one would indicate the country doesn't carry more risk than the average for all countries so would be a safe bet. Betas of less than one means the individual country index will fluctuate less than the global index. From 2008, betas both above and below one were evenly split between developing and emerging economies.

Investing internationally can be made via funds. Investing across a broad spectrum of a country's sectors can be achieved with WEBS (World Equity Benchmark Series). Individual shares of a country can be bought through ADRs (American Depository Receipts), which are held in the currency of origin. This is useful for investors who want exposure to a currency, and who believe it offers a better currency hedge. However, diversification benefits are lost by holding individual shares, as opposed to a fund. For passive investors that want a broad-based portfolio, investing in a global fund is an option. It should be noted that there is disagreement within the investing community as to whether diversifying internationally offers any noticeable benefits. Another observation is that during periods of global turbulence international markets converge so lose benefits derived from diversification.

Portfolio Examples

A portfolio comprises all the assets owned by an investor, structured in such a way to reflect attitudes towards risk, age, goals and so on. It should be remembered that asset allocation is the single most important investment process comprising 90% of returns. So how you allocate between classes in more important than the selection of them, or timing. The two main assets classes are equities and bonds. The greater the level of equities to bonds the greater the risk and, hopefully, the reward. The greater the percentage of bonds held in a portfolio, the lower the risk. Typically, younger investors will be more aggressive, holding a higher percentage of equities to grow their pile, whereas retirees will be conservative having less opportunity to recover from major downturns. They will veer, therefore, towards a greater percentage held in bonds. Moving an imaginary slider between aggressive and conservative reveals the range of allocations from risky to risk free and from higher to stable returns

A portfolio split between 60% in equities and 40% in bonds has been the benchmark portfolio against which investors will cling to one degree or another. Equities provide growth while bonds hedge risk when equities become volatile. In more recent times, bonds have not provided as much shelter since they now tend to move in the same direction, up or down, with equities. This may be partly due to the low interest rate environment that has pushed up bond values, making them attractive for their potential gains. The other downside is that investors who depend on fixed income products like bonds are not being adequately rewarded. This has compelled many to invest in riskier assets in search of yield, often at the expense of maintaining 60/40 asset allocation. Nevertheless, this balance has held true under most market conditions so offers a starting place for most investors. The final allocation may vary somewhat.

Within the 60/40 allocation, equities may be split between local and international, and bonds may be split between corporate bonds and governments bonds, including municipal bonds. In addition to these two assets classes, it is not uncommon to find small allocations to real estate and 'alternative' investments. Real estate may be split between REITs, which trade like shares and often move with them, and direct ownership, which will be less correlated to markets. Alternatives cover a gamut of investments some of which will not be suitable for retail investors. Examples of alternatives are private equity, derivatives, infrastructure, forest, land, art and antiques, and commodities.

Gold is a commodity and often forms part of retail investors portfolios, but is rarely a permanent allocation since it provides no income and—some argue—has no intrinsic value. Infrastructure may hold some promise as it is real estate and provides stable cash flow, and some inflation hedging. Private equity is often leveraged, and forests etc are illiquid. The drive towards alternatives has come about as institutional investors seek to add back diversification into portfolios where asset classes have become increasingly correlated. The Yale Endowment fund holds over 70% of its assets in alternatives. It is perhaps unsurprising that bond allocations are being sacrificed for exposure to alternatives. This process is known as 'financial repression', and has meant pension funds have had to forsake disproportionately higher levels of capital to meet their obligations. Pension funds are obligated to be invested in bonds.

Surprisingly, given the importance of asset allocation, finding officially recommended portfolios are hard to come by. Neither the SEC (Securities and Exchange Commission), which regulates financial markets, nor FINRA that oversees brokers offer any models. PIMFA, a leading financial trade association in the UK does offer portfolio models, which it categorizes as conservative, income, balanced and growth. While they are specific to the UK market, they may be useful as a reference or guide. There are some portfolio calculators online that use different parameters to determine asset allocation, but they are not sophisticated and should not be relied upon. Morningstar offers a form of analysis based on virtual portfolios that can be created on their website. It will suggest areas that have over-exposure or under-exposure, and suitability based on investing time horizon, but it tends to offer blanket answers so isn't useful on specifics. Portfoliovisualizer offers possibly the most comprehensive portfolio suggestions based on a range of theoretical underpinnings. It also gives ticker symbols to illustrate these models, but investors would be advised to do their own due diligence rather than taking them at face value. Other portfolio suggestions can be found in the abundant literature available. Below are a few examples drawn from multiple sources:

Two Fund Portfolio
60% Equities (broadly diversified passive index fund)
40% Bonds (broadly diversified actively managed fund)

Three Fund Portfolio
40% Domestic equities
20% International equities
40% Bonds

Typical Portfolio
30% Domestic equities
20% International equities
15% Real estate
15% Inflation linked bonds (TIPS)
15% Bonds
 5% Cash

Broader Exposure
30% Domestic equity
15% International equity (developed economies)
 5% Emerging market equities
20% Real Estate
15% US treasuries
15% TIPS

Allocation with Alternatives
17.5% Domestic equities
15% International equities
10% Government bonds
22.5% Corporate bonds
 7.5% Inflation-linked bonds
 7.5% Cash
20% Alternatives

Income
25% Equities
29% Bonds
  8% High Yield bonds
  8% Emerging economies
10% REITs
15% TIPS
  5% Cash

Recession
46% Domestic equity
  4% International equity
  4% International bonds
46% Government bonds

Volatility Hedge
20% Domestic equities
20% Small Cap equities
60% Short term government bonds

When markets are volatile and in decline, rolling out of equities and into bonds, especially short maturity government bonds make sense. However, more exposure to bonds inevitably entails losing out on the growth that equities provide. One theory is to allocate the equity allocation between value and small cap equities. Small cap and value equities are said to be negatively correlated and outperform the market over the long haul. If the investor can ride the highs and lows inherent within them, and has an outsized allocation to government bonds (60-80%), the portfolio may offer greater protection to the downside. Again, in a low interest rate environment government bonds may offer a sense of security, but they do not provide investors with the yields of yesteryear. They also will be exposed to declines in value when interest rates rise.

When devising a suitable portfolio, care needs to be taken there is no overlap between allocations. For example, international equities may already have domestic exposure, and some well-diversified funds may already have real estate exposure. Bond funds may include both corporate and governments bonds. For portfolios with five or more different categories, it is recommended to keep allocations between 30% and 5% for each category. Given the vast array of possible portfolio mixes, it is important to remain anchored to personal goals and circumstances. The simple precept that equities add growth but increase volatility needs balancing with bonds that shelter against volatility while offering dependable income. Younger investors will be overweight equities, and older investors overweight bonds. The risk averse investor during severe downturns will liquidate securities for the security of cash.

The use of backtesting can help determine the ongoing viability of a portfolio. Using historical data, backtesting performs an analysis of financial indicators such as total return, standard deviation, and maximum drawdowns. By going back in time, the investor can see how well, or poorly a portfolio performed over a given period. Portfoliovisualizer offers a backtest facility.

Modern-Day Challenges

The following text draws attention to a few issues that impact financial decisions. Bubbles have been with us for a long time so are nothing new. However, over the last two decades since 2000, we have seen two major bubbles burst. At the time of writing, asset valuations remain elevated and some say are in bubble territory. While Covid-19 works its way through the system, it remains to be seen whether markets will eventually capitulate, leading to a similar market unwind we saw in both 2001 and 2008. Bubbles and over-valuations present a challenge to all investors and risk models used by investors have not caught up with recent events. Recovery times favor younger investors, while older investors depending on investments to supplement pensions can't afford to make the wrong decisions. What does all this mean, and how can investors navigate these choppy waters?

A first step is being aware of behavioral traits we looked at in Chapter 3. We often behave in ways that seem intuitive, but which can harm our interests. Perhaps more important is gaining an understanding of the risk-reward relationship and the benefits of diversification. In addition, there is increasing speculation about whether markets are functioning efficiently. On a more fundamental level, it is important to understand the broader context of the investing environment, how economic and financial factors sometimes appear to be at odds with each other. A growing concern is the apparent greater dislocation between the

two, that seems to be driven largely by policy decisions, both fiscal and monetary.

Markets have become very attuned, or 'addicted' to
stimulus from central banks. Understanding how
changes in interest rates impact financial markets and
the economy helps in shaping future expectations and
investing decisions. It is equally important to understand that policy goals don't always lead to intended
outcomes. The effect of pumping large amount of liquidity into the system has had the unintended consequences of the misallocation of capital. Companies
have refrained from investing in productivity, prefer-
ring to focus on financial engineering. The large increase in the money supply may eventually lead to inflation. In August, 2020, the Federal Reserve Bank indicated it was prepared to let inflation increase above
its target rate to make up for years of below target inflation.

The low costs of borrowing has encouraged increasingly higher levels of personal, private and public
debt. The main risks are from interest rates when they
move upwards, and from default risk as debt obligations come under pressure. This can threaten the
economy with systemic risk that can have catastrophic
consequences. Another threat is from inflation and deflation. Inflationary pressures lead to monetary tightening, in which interest rates rise pushing down asset
values. This becomes particularly germane when asset
values have become very inflated by extended periods
of monetary easing. Elevated levels of borrowing may
compel governments to raise taxes to pay down their

debt, while the corporate sector may engage in deleveraging lowering their prospects for future growth. Fearing tax increases to pay down increasing government debt, consumers will tighten their own fiscal belts putting more downward pressure on economies.

Following the collapse of credit markets in 2008, the growth of CDOs (Collateralized Debt Obligations) was significantly impaired. However, concerns have resurfaced that high levels of student debt and relaxed lending standards in auto loans are at risk of defaulting. Another area where debt poses a risk is in the corporate world. Business, unable to raise capital in conventional markets have sought financing through leveraged loans. These loans have been collateralized and sold on mirroring the securitization of subprime mortgage debt. Some investors fear this could lead to another credit crisis. Credit rating agencies point out that the collateralization of leveraged loans (CLOs) are sufficiently diversified across the risk spectrum that they don't present a danger to investors. It should be remembered that credit rating agencies were blamed for their role in the crisis of 2008. It became apparent that a conflict of interest lay at the heart of the relationship between agencies and their *de facto* clients, the corporations. Rating agencies depended on their income from the very companies they rated. Investors would be wise to watch this space for further cracks in the armor. A worst-case scenario is that lending freezes if banks stop lending to each other for fear of being exposed to toxic debt.

Following the credit crisis, lending regulations were tightened culminating in the Dodd-Frank Act in 2010, that overhauled much of the financial system. In 2018, there has been a rolling back of parts of the Act as financial companies have complained it stifled competition. Placing these events into a historical context is revealing. The repeal of the Glass-Steagall Act in 1999, by President Bill Clinton is sometimes blamed for the financial crises that followed. The Act was brought into being in response to the Great Depression. It prevented commercial banks from being involved in investment banking. Whatever the case for or against, investors need to be aware of the shifting regulatory framework as it tightens and relaxes its grip on financial markets. When the regulatory ethos favors a relaxed environment, innovation will follow but so will excess risk taking. When rules become restrictive is creates disincentives and lowers growth expectations, but will include consumer protections.

Globalization is a term that refers to an increasing interconnectedness of economies and business around the world. To remain competitive, Western companies have sought ways to reduce costs by outsourcing to countries where labor is cheaper. This outsourcing is not confined to unskilled labor. Jobs that require a high level of skills such as software development and pharmaceuticals have also been affected. The impact on unemployment in those countries that have aggressively outsourced labor has been negative, creating a politically charged environment. In the US, it has led to trade wars with China following the election of Donald Trump as president in 2016. While trade wars are generally considered to have little positive outcome for either side, they create uncertainty for businesses and financial markets.

Classical economic theory claims trading relationships are straight forward, but the reality is business transactions can be complex, involving considerable costs as they relate to bargaining, monitoring and enforcing contracts. Nowhere was this more evident than in the competing arguments for and against the departure of the UK from EU referred to as Brexit and formally ratified in 2020. Consequently, financial markets in the UK including the British Pound, were delivered a severe blow. With the onset of Covid-19, the UK faced a double whammy and a bleak outlook. Policy makers had not only miscalculated sentiment, they had also failed to consider the macro environment. The economic cycle was already in its late stages and showing signs of slowing down. Investors needed to assess the increased risk that these two major events combined posed to their assets. Taking decisions retroactively can have lasting consequences, so weighing up how markets will react, given what is known at the time, can help with formulating an appropriate response. For example, paring back exposure to sectors most affected, or more broadly reducing risk. In the case of Brexit, larger corporations were economically exposed more than SMEs, because they conducted more business within the EU.

While globalization has its advocates and critics alike, global warming and climate change has seen countries around the world acknowledge that cooperation is not a choice but a necessity. Predictions by scientists of the catastrophic humanitarian and economic consequences of ignoring the unfolding disaster has instilled fear and given rise to contention. Governments are torn between short term goals and the growing realization of consequences looming over the horizon if left unchecked. It is clear a partnership between private and public sectors holds out the best hope. Massive reductions in the use of fossil fuels are needed to avert disaster. The race for developing alternative sources of energy sufficient to replace the huge demand for energy has not kept pace with the encroaching problem. It seems likely a solution will reside in a combination of disaster management and technology.

Glimmers of hope for solutions to climate change are surfacing as there is increasing public and investor pressure on companies to adapt to the changes. Corporate governance is more and more embracing moral dimensions in answer to tensions over environmental issues. The investing world, too, has seen a move towards a culture of social awareness and public good. It is now possible to invest in ESG (Environmental, Social and Governance) funds and ETFs, that reflect the investment community's need to be on board. The US government's actions to stymie this mood is reprehensible. More still needs to be done to encourage research and investment in alternative energy sources. The investment community appears muted in its approach to investing in this area so far, but this may change and offer attractive opportunities in the not-too-distant future. Much will depend on changes in attitudes.

Chasing Yield
This is unquestionably one of the biggest challenges for many investors, especially those who depend on fixed incomes from investments. Open market operations known as quantitative easing, or QE, drives bond rates down to such low levels, it pushes investors into higher risk assets in search of better returns. The challenge is trying to obtain acceptable yields while minimizing risk. This has skewed portfolios towards more risk for a mere percentage point or two in increased returns. Enhanced income can be obtained from products such as multi-sector bond funds, floating rate bonds, agency loans, infrastructure, MLPs, REITs, high yield (junk) bonds, dividend stocks, municipal bonds, callable bonds, preferred stock, real estate, CD and bond ladders, and crowdfunding.

When buying bonds in a ladder, higher rates are captured by staggering maturity dates over the duration of the ladder. As bonds mature they can be reinvested at better rates. Buying bonds at par ensures you are reimbursed the full amount of the investment. Floating rate bonds are better in a rising rate environment. Callable bonds may be recalled when interest rates are lowered. Care needs to be taken with high yield. It is not called 'junk' for no reason. Investing in a high yield bond fund with a good rating is advisable. MLPs are legal entities that pay out a high percentage of their underlying income. They are associated largely with natural resources such as oil so will be exposed to the vagaries of that sector. They also have tax implications so consult a professional before investing in them.

Agency loans refer to GSEs (Government Sponsored Entities), which are semi-autonomous bodies and underwrite large segments of the mortgage market. They are relatively risk free providing some stability for the yield-chasing investor. Their existence does court controversy with some policy makers, who call for their disbandment believing the mortgage market would benefit from a broader participation.

With all fixed income investments, being cognizant of central bank interest rate policy and broad economic indicators such as inflation and growth will help guide the choice of investment. Low interest rates may signal to markets that central banks are being accommodative, but if asset prices rise well beyond intrinsic values the shadow of downside risk looms ominously as economic growth depresses expectations of earnings growth. Should the economy show signs of over-heating, it can be expected inflation will follow and interest rates will be raised to contain it.

Conflicts of Interest
Agency theory claims managers act it the interests of shareholders, but as shareholders often own only a small fraction of a company, their knowledge of operations and control is limited. This means managers can act more or less with impunity. Incentivizing managers by rewarding them with share options should ensure that shareholder and manager interests are aligned. However, dividends paid to shareholders will reduce the value of their shares so managers will be less inclined to distribute them. Instead, they are more inclined to reward investors with share buybacks, which

reduce the number of shares outstanding increasing earnings per share. That clearly benefits managers who see an increase in the value of their share options. Shareholders may feel that excess cash used for buying back shares could have been put to more productive use. The focus on the short term and maximizing shareholder value may deter possible takeovers, but may also detract from long term needs of companies to remain competitive, ultimately hurting shareholders' interests.

We've seen conflicts of interest occur with credit rating agencies and companies. We also see it with analytical models that present overly rosy forecasts of future earnings. An area of direct concern to investors is the conflict created by commission-driven incentives. Financial advisors are sometimes paid higher commissions to push a particular product, even if the product is neither needed, nor appropriate, nor performs particularly well. Fees based on performance may encourage financial advisers to take on undue risk.

Pension Plans
For the last two to three decades, pension plans have moved away from the more traditional schemes, known as defined benefit plans provided by companies, towards defined contribution plans that place responsibility for investing with employees. The reason for this shift was that companies found the task of calculating pensions onerous. Holding pensions on balance sheets also tended to distort financial reporting. Consultants needed to maintain the provision of pensions was also costly distracting management from

core operations. Passing on responsibility for investing to employees was a way to avoid these issues. Quite how individuals are expected to perform the complex task of investing for retirement better than corporations with all their resources is a mystery.

In the UK, this shift of responsibility led to claims of 'mis-selling'. The plans on offer were commission driven, overly optimistic about future returns, and poorly conceived, leading to lost savings for many investors. Perhaps not unsurprisingly, in the US and the UK retirees are more likely to live below the poverty line than is France and Germany, where the responsibility for pension planning is not placed with the individual.

High Frequency Trading and Dark Pools
Computers have made it possible to conduct trading of securities at very fast speeds. Profits are made by exploiting tiny differences in stock prices, being the differences between the bid and ask price known as the spread. Competition is so fierce that traders will move their offices to be as close to the exchanges as possible to gain millisecond electronic trading advantages. Some large investors have complained they are placed at a disadvantage because high frequency traders appear to know in advance what they are going to do.

Large trades are often obscured from view to avoid attracting too much attention. They have the somewhat sinister name "dark pool" and can distort pricing for other investors. Large trades are sometimes broken up into much smaller trades with the aim of hiding the transaction. With this degree of sophistication and behind-the-scenes murky operations, individual investors may be forgiven for feeling the odds are stacked against them. High frequency traders, on the other hand, will claim their activities help maintain price equilibrium.

Short Selling
Short selling is a strategy for making a profit when an investor thinks the shares of a company are very likely to decline in value. Shares are sold at the current price and then bought back when they have fallen in value. The profit is the difference between the original price and the new lower price. To make things more complicated, the short-seller first borrows the shares from a broker who has borrowed them from someone else, such as a client. He or she gives some money as security to the broker in case the shares go up in value instead of down. This is placed in a margin account, and the broker may ask for more money, a margin call, if things get wobbly. Once the shares have declined in value, they are bought back and returned to the original owner, often without their knowledge of the transactions.

The process sounds a little underhand, and it has its detractors. Many claim short selling contributes to financial crises because share prices can be adversely affected. There are occasions when it has been banned in the US and the UK. It was banned altogether is Australia. However, there are many investors, including academics, who believe that it is an efficient process in the sense that markets are re-pricing shares that may be over-valued. Naked short selling occurs when shares are not even borrowed, and haven't even been proved to exist yet are sold. When it comes time to return the shares that should have been borrowed, the investor hopes he can source them in the market. It is a high-risk strategy and questions remain over the legality of the practice.

'Short interest' measures how much shorting activity there is for a given stock, so is a useful guide as to how short sellers view valuations. If there is a lot of short interest activity it means traders anticipate values to fall. At the time of writing short interest was high for major technology companies, and given their extreme valuations against the recessionary backdrop of Covid-19, it comes as no surprise. Investors may wish to add this measure to their arsenal of fundamental analysis tools.

Moral Hazard
Moral hazard comes about when poor behavior is given the incentive to continue. If you reward someone for doing something questionable, they will continue doing it. If bailing out industries and pumping liquidity into the system is what drives economies out of crises, then moral hazard is the exhaust that pollutes and obscures in the aftermath. While the notion of moral hazard is not new, its relevance in recent years is increasingly apparent, especially in the financial sector. Prior to the credit crisis in 2008, banks' balance sheets had become systematically weaker. They did not have sufficient assets to cover liabilities so faced

solvency issues. Governments assisted by injecting money into them to keep them solvent. Regulation then stepped in to ensure capital buffers were sufficient to counteract future extreme events.

The source of banks' problems can be traced back to interbank lending, which provides short term liquidity. If a bank over-extends itself, other banks won't lend to it. Depositors then become fearful and withdraw their savings. This is called a 'run' on the bank, and as fear escalates more savings are withdrawn. A bank may find it does not have the funds available to service all the large number of requests for cash so will face insolvency.

During the 2008-09 crisis, regulation tackled the problem of insufficient reserves, and depositor insurance (FDIC) gave account holders peace of mind knowing they would not lose their money if their banks became insolvent. With checking and savings accounts secured by insurance, people would be less likely to withdraw their money keeping banks solvent. But with a government guarantee and insurance there is no incentive for banks to change their behavior. In some senses, we see this moral hazard playing out in financial markets that have become dependent on central bank monetary easing. Speculation can run amok with the knowledge Fed accommodation will calm markets when they become volatile.

While Basel III has gone someway to protect against insolvency and the potential for systemic risk, capital requirements are likely to bite into earnings, possibly leading to pressure from banks for a gradual loosening of regulations. Investors need to be aware of these issues and keep their fingers on the pulse where regulation and moral hazard are concerned, as they can have dire consequences for investing and the economy at large. When regulation fails to tackle issues after a crisis, the foundations for a repeat crisis are already laid. When price discovery is not functioning as it should, distortions make for an unforgiving investment environment.

Conclusion

The opening chapter of this book was based on the idea that for many investors passive investing in funds that track the broad market offer an easy solution. Doing away with the need for complex analysis and decisions associated with investing is clearly a major plus. Index funds offer the necessary diversification to reduce risk, and are low cost so compete with managed funds in terms of overall returns. Since asset allocation provides the lion's share of returns, a simple two fund portfolio split of 60:40 between equities and bonds is a one-size-fits-all solution. All things being equal, that should be all most investors need to do. However, other factors such as human behavior, asset bubbles, unforeseen events, economic conditions, policy responses, conflicts of interest, and regulations still need to be considered. Low interest rates, extended bull markets, increasing levels of debt, globalization, and trade conflicts all add to uncertainty. The heightened uncertainty of recent decades, challenges traditional risk models and strategies for investing. Investors can no longer rely on strategies of the past, and need to be more aware of the changing landscape. Through a better understanding of how markets are being shaped and molded, investors can adapt to the new challenges.

As the current Covid-19 pandemic unfolds, predictions of a severe impact on economies are widespread, yet markets remain optimistic leading many to question how disconnected they are from the fundamentals. With valuations teetering at record levels the stakes are high. This creates an acute sensitivity to deteriorating conditions, but also to policy responses especially from central banks. For investors, questions remain regarding the continued effectiveness of monetary and fiscal stimulus. If their effectiveness dwindles, will a liquidity trap emerge, a process likened to pushing on a string. If that point arrives, it is conceivable financial markets will spiral downwards. While that could be catastrophic, we can take some comfort that historically markets do eventually recover and offer opportunities in the process. It doesn't, however, offer much hope that we will see an end to the troubling trend of boom-bust cycles. If markets are broken, perhaps an alternative will emerge taking advantage of technological innovation allowing companies alternatives to raise capital and investors to invest more directly. Perhaps a reduction in the level of intermediation will bring more stability to markets making them accessible to a wider range of individuals wishing to invest. We can only hope.

Useful Websites

Finance
www.morningstar.com *Data/Ratings*
https://www.portfoliovisualizer.com/ *Online Tools (Optimization)*
https://finance.google.com/finance *Data*
https://finance.yahoo.com/ *Data*
https://seekingalpha.com/ *Discussions*
https://www.standardandpoors.com/en_US/web/guest/home *Ratings*
https://www.betterment.com/ *Robo Advisor*
https://unicornbay.com/main *Robo Advisor*
https://www.csi.ca/student/en_ca/home.xhtml *Education*
http://www.cboe.com/ *Options Exchange*
https://markets.cboe.com/us/options/market_statistics/daily/ *Volatility*
https://www.marketwatch.com/investing/index/vix/charts *Volatility*
https://www.marketinout.com/chart/market.php?breadth=advance-decline-line *Momentum*
https://www.aaii.com/ *Sentiment*
https://www.optionseducation.org/ *Options*
https://www.optionsprofitcalculator.com/calculator/long-put.html *Options Calculator*
https://www.cfainstitute.org/en *Education*
https://www.investing.com/ *General*
https://stockcharts.com/ *Charts*
https://money.cnn.com/data/markets/ *News*
https://markets.ft.com/data/ *Analytics*
https://www.ft.com/ *News*

https://www.msci.com/ *Analytics*
https://www.pimfa.co.uk/ *Trade Body*
https://www.ishares.com/us *ETFs*
https://www.multpl.com/shiller-pe/table/by-year/ *CAPE Ratio*
https://www.dividendchannel.com/ *Analytics*
https://www.proshares.com/ *Funds*
https://www.fintools.com/ *Online Calculators*
https://www.etfreplay.com/ *ETFs*
https://www.etfscreen.com/ *ETFs*
https://www.tradingview.com/ *General*
https://www.thebalance.com/ *General*

Economy
http://www.econstats.com/
https://www.gapminder.org/ *Fun tools/demographics*
https://data.london.gov.uk/
https://www.aeaweb.org/rfe/
https://www.worldbank.org/
https://www.imf.org/external/index.htm
https://www.ons.gov.uk/
https://www.conference-board.org/data/bci.cfm *Indicators*
https://www.bls.gov/ *Data*
https://fred.stlouisfed.org/ *Data*
https://fred.stlouisfed.org/series/BAMLC0A0CM *Corporate Bond Spread*
https://www.calculatedriskblog.com/ *Data*

Real Estate
https://fundrise.com/ *Crowdfunding*
https://www.biggerpockets.com/ *Forums*

https://www.ncreif.org/ *Commercial Real Estate*
http://www.acadata.co.uk/
https://www.redfin.com/blog/data-center/
https://www.redfin.com/blog/real-estate-news/
https://fred.stlouisfed.org/series/csushpinsa *Home Prices*
https://realestatedecoded.com/case-shiller/ *Home Prices*
https://www.nar.realtor/ *Data*
https://www.nar.realtor/research-and-statistics/housing-statistics/housing-affordability-index
https://www.fhfa.gov/DataTools/Downloads/Pages/House-Price-Index.aspx
https://www.gov.uk/search-house-prices *Home Prices UK*

Other
https://www.artprice.com/ *Art*
https://www.cfainstitute.org/ *Qualifications*
https://www.investopedia.com/ Information

References

Mazzucato, Lowe, Shipman, Trigg. Personal Investment: Financial Planning in an Uncertain World. Palgrave Macmillan, 2010. Open University, UK

Model Team Open University, Introduction to Corporate Finance. Open University, 2016

Bodie, Kane, Marcus. Essentials of Investments. McGraw-Hill & Irwin, 2013
Module Team Open University, Doing Economics, Open University, UK. 2013

Barbara Rockefeller, Technical Analysis For Dummies, John Wiley & Sons, 2014

Sean Cook, Investing in Real Estate Private Equity, Amazon, 2016

Benjamin Graham (Jason Zweig), The Intelligent Investor (Revised Edition), Harpers-Collins.

David Swensen, Unconventional Success: A Fundamental Approach to Personal Investment, Free Press

Harvey, Gall, Kangas, Modern Real Estate Investing: The Delaware Statutory Trust, Cornerstone, 2018

Joe Duarte, Trading Options For Dummies, John Wiley, 2017

Larry Swedroe & Kevin Grogan, Reducing the Risk of Black Swans, Bam Alliance, 2018
Index

Investopedia, Several references throughout the book,

Open University, Masters in Finance, Online Course Material

Michel Sincere, Understanding Options (2nd Edition), McGraw-Hill, 2014

9 798683 864064